"This beautifully written book provides a compelling account of why the main aim of western education is to cultivate the capacity to reason, and how the meaning and educational importance of this aim has changed over time in response to changing historical conditions. Wilfred Carr makes a strong case for the need to revive and reclaim this educational aim in the social and political climate that exists today."

Fazal Rizvi, *Emeritus Professor, University of Melbourne Australia*

"This book explains how cultivating our ability to reason became the unique purpose of Western education and how this purpose has been eroded by the recent establishment of mass schooling and the pervasive character of neoliberalism. Carr concisely outlines the history of this conception of education and draws on a range of historically important educational philosophies to argue that there is the urgent need for educators to reclaim it for today."

Professor Eleanore Hargreaves, *Faculty of Education and Society, University College London, UK*

The Eclipse of Reason

This concise, digestible book shows how the cultivation of reason became the defining aim of western education, and critiques how this aim has been eclipsed in recent decades by the neoliberal system of mass schooling imposed by the state.

Chapters outline succinctly the history of western education and its origins in Ancient Greece, demonstrating how the idea of education as intrinsically related to the development of reason became embedded in the Western educational tradition, and how this tradition subsequently developed and evolved. Introducing key philosophical ideas about the nature of education, the book shows how the development of mass schooling in the 19th century led to our current educational landscape, where neoliberal demands for schools to be more responsive to market forces have obscured the development of reason as a distinctive educational aim. By inviting educators to think reflectively and critically about the state of education today, the book raises the little-discussed educational question of what comes after neoliberalism.

Calling for the re-establishment of western education's core values and aims, this book will be of interest to educators, researchers and students involved with pre- and in-service teacher education courses, as well as those interested in the history of education and the philosophy of education more broadly.

Wilfred Carr is Emeritus Professor of Education, University of Sheffield, UK.

Routledge Research in Education

This series aims to present the latest research from right across the field of education. It is not confined to any particular area or school of thought and seeks to provide coverage of a broad range of topics, theories and issues from around the world.

State of Primary Education in Bhutan
Culture, Development and Innovation
Edited by Gembo Tshering

Research-Practice Partnerships in Education
Practitioner-Researcher Collaboration in the Israeli Context
Edited by Linor L. Hadar and Hadar Baharav

Quiet Classrooms, Educational Soundscapes, and the Power of Silence
Towards an Acoustic History of Education
Pieter Verstraete

Commercialising Public Schooling
Practices of Profit-Making
Anna Hogan

The Eclipse of Reason
Reclaiming Western Education for Today
Wilfred Carr

For more information about this series, please visit: www.routledge.com/Routledge-Research-in-Education/book-series/SE0393

The Eclipse of Reason

Reclaiming Western Education for Today

Wilfred Carr

LONDON AND NEW YORK

First published 2025
by Routledge
4 Park Square, Milton Park, Abingdon, Oxon OX14 4RN

and by Routledge
605 Third Avenue, New York, NY 10158

Routledge is an imprint of the Taylor & Francis Group, an informa business

British Library Cataloguing-in-Publication Data
A catalogue record for this book is available from the British Library

ISBN: 978-1-041-03860-3 (hbk)
ISBN: 978-1-041-03862-7 (pbk)
ISBN: 978-1-003-62573-5 (ebk)

DOI: 10.4324/9781003625735

Typeset in Times New Roman
by Newgen Publishing UK

FOR

Alys, Huw, Samuel, Theodore and Wilfred

Contents

Preface *xi*

1 Introduction: Understanding Education 1

2 The Birth of Reason and the Origins of Education 8

3 Antiquity: The Formation of the Western Educational Tradition 18

4 Christianity: The Decline and Revival of the Western Educational Tradition 32

5 The Enlightenment and the Emergence of Progressive Education 44

6 Education and State Schooling 53

7 Democracy and Education 61

8 Education Today: The Demise of the Western Educational Tradition 75

9 Conclusion: Reclaiming Education for Today 84

Index *89*

Preface

The initial aim of this book was to provide a short history of education that would be of interest to a wide audience, as well as students studying education in colleges and universities. But this simple intention was soon complicated by the fact that I also wanted it to provide, as far as possible, some understanding of the state of education in our own modern times. In particular, I wanted it to speak to, and for, all those parents, teachers and other educational professionals who have serious misgivings about the way that education is now organised and conducted and suspect that they have been coerced into accepting a view of education that they feel intuitively reluctant to accept or endorse.

The way I have pursued this aim has also been affected by my long-standing concerns about how and why the English education system fell victim to the impoverished understanding of education imposed on it by the numerous educational changes introduced by successive conservative governments in the 1970s and 1980s. My efforts to understand the causes and consequences of these changes have led me to reach three conclusions, all of which are firmly embodied in this book. The first is that the adverse educational effects of these changes largely arise from the extent to which they embody the ethos of our modern age. The second is that it is only by rejecting a large part of this ethos that we can recover a more rationally compelling educational viewpoint from which the inadequacies of present-day education can be critically exposed. The third, and more perturbing, conclusion is that the all-pervasive influence of this ethos has been sufficient to deprive teachers and other educational professionals of any adequate theoretical or practical understanding of education to which they can give their allegiance and from which they can make sense of their distinctively *educational* role. The aim of this book is to make this understanding available.

These conclusions are not necessarily shared by my friend and colleague Stephen Kemmis, whose influence on this book has been continual from the time that the idea for this book was first muted to its final completion. In our numerous discussions of early drafts of the book, Stephen's ability to combine just criticism with constructive advice has, on many occasions, led me to rewrite something I had written or rethink something I had said. For this, I can only offer my gratitude and thanks. I also owe a great debt of gratitude to my academic colleagues, Pádraig Hogan and Ansgar Allen, whose generous and incisive comments on earlier drafts of the manuscript have made this a better book than it would otherwise have been. I must also thank my close friend John Chadfield who provided me with invaluable comments about the argument of of the book and how it could be made accessible to a non-academic audience. I am also grateful to the six anonymous reviewers who assessed my original book proposal and made important recommendations about how it could be improved. Finally, I must thank AnnaMary Goodall and Kanishka Jangir at Routledge for all their help in seeing my original book proposal through to eventual publication.

1 Introduction

Understanding Education

This book emerged from extended reflections on the inadequacies of our modern understanding of education and from a growing frustration with our inability to detect the distortions to educational thought and practice to which these inadequacies have given rise. What these reflections have led me to conclude is that we have largely lost our ability to ask fundamental questions about what education actually is, and so are incapable of knowing whether what we now call 'education' is education in any proper sense at all. To make this disturbing conclusion even more unsettling, I have also become increasingly conscious of the fact that many – though not all – of those who have suffered this loss do not realise what has been erased from their memory. Unable to recall the conception of education to which they had previously given their allegiance, many schools, colleges and universities no longer feel compelled to defend themselves as genuinely *educational* institutions or distinguish themselves from institutions that are not. And, unaware of the distinctively educational standpoint that would previously have allowed them to justify their practices as *educational* practices, many teachers now lack any understanding of themselves as professional *educators* and can only make sense of what and how they teach in instrumental terms: as the means to ends that are extrinsic to education itself.

But if we have now largely lost our ability to think and act in distinctively educational terms, how can this incapacity be overcome? The argument running throughout this book is that the most appropriate way to retrieve what has been lost is to bring our contemporary understanding of education face to face with its own history. Indeed, unless we are prepared to bring our present view of education into

DOI: 10.4324/9781003625735-1

critical confrontation with the different ways it has been understood in the past, we will not only be unable to detect any distortions that may be infecting how education is now being practised and understood. We will also remain blind to the possibility that our present understanding may be the end product of a long historical process through which an older, more coherent and more compelling understanding of education has been abandoned and disowned.

Constructing a historical narrative that will enable us to recognise the parochial nature of our present-day understanding of education is complicated by the fact that there is no history of education 'as such' or 'in general.' There are the histories of Asian education, Indian education and Islamic education, but a history of education that is not embedded in some particular cultural context is nowhere to be found. Since the purpose of this book is to illuminate how education is understood in our own modern culture, it will inevitably focus on the history of what is usually referred to as 'Western education.'

What, within our Western culture, is the history of education the history of? What is education *for*? The answer permeating every page of this book is that when true to its own historical mission, the unique and particular purpose of Western education is to cultivate what is the defining characteristic of humanity: the ability to reason. This view of education is predicated on an obvious truth: that, by nurturing the power of human reason, education transforms human beings from irrational slaves to innate impulses and desires into rational animals who are able to shape their beliefs, emotions, feelings and actions on the basis of their own rational reflections and critical thought. It is through education so understood that individuals are able to think critically and creatively and to differentiate what is true from what is false and what is right from what is wrong. It is what makes it possible for us to deliberate, discuss and choose, to engage in argument and debate, to evaluate our emotions and feelings and to resolve our disagreements and conflicts in a rationally defensible way. And it is by exercising the power of reason that we are able to transcend the rational inadequacies of our opinions and beliefs and so free ourselves from prejudices, dogmas and superstitions we may have inherited from the past. It is this concern with the development of reason that explains why, in the Western world, education is always regarded as the antithesis of indoctrination and very different from narrow vocational training. It also explains why 'education' is not treated as synonymous with 'schooling,' an insight neatly captured by the American writer Mark Twain when he advised his friend to 'take care your son's schooling doesn't interfere with his education.'

About the kind of reason that education serves to cultivate, I want to stress four things. First, it is not restricted to rationality in a narrow logical sense; it is also about reasonableness, being open to reason, listening to the arguments of others and being willing to consider different points of view. Second, it is very different from the instrumental reasoning we use to calculate the most effect means to achieving some given end but is incapable of rationally determining what these ends should be. Third, the ability to reason serves nothing except itself, no one except those who exercise it; it demands independence of mind; no one can be rational on someone else's behalf. Finally, since we are all equal before the impersonal standards of reason, the capacity to reason cannot, by its very nature, be the prerogative of an elite. Throughout history, the ability to reason has been made the exclusive preserve of some special class, usually a privileged white male aristocracy, from which other groups – women, ethnic minorities and others – have been excluded. To create such an elite is to allow one social group to debase rational standards for everyone else. And to allow this is to convert reason into an ideological weapon to be used by some to maintain power and control over others.

It also needs to be pointed out that to claim that the aim of education is to cultivate the ability to reason is not to suggest that education is some kind of neutral instrument by means of which this aim can be effectively 'delivered' or 'produced.' Rather, it is simply to insist that any teaching practice can only be made intelligible as a genuinely *educational* practice if it itself gives expression to the rational values (intellectual honesty, respect for the truth, impartiality, tolerance willingness to engage in discussion and argument and the like) that the ability to reason presupposes and requires. It is only by tacitly appealing to these values that it is possible to distinguish forms of teaching and learning that are conducive to the cultivation of reason from more mundane attempts to instil instrumental knowledge or technical skills. And it is by reference to these values that any teaching practices that deprive learners of their ability to rationally determine their beliefs and actions can be seen to serve no distinctively *educational* purpose at all. In this sense, the aim of education and the means for its realisation are intrinsically related. Each constitutes, and is itself constituted by, the other.

How is the history of this understanding of education to be written? What first we would expect this history to reveal is how, in the transition from one historical period to another, the way this understanding of education was being interpreted changed. We can also except it to emphasise those occasions when these changes were assisted by the arguments of influential individuals who – convinced that the kind of education prevalent in their own culture was hindering, rather than promoting, the development of reason – articulated an 'educational philosophy' that led to education being interpreted and conducted in a fundamentally different way. Because the idea of education as the development of reason has, since its inception, been amenable to this kind of philosophical reconstruction, its history is both a history of continuity and a history of change. And it is because educational practices and institutions always implicitly embody ideas and arguments derived from some educational philosophy that the history of these practices and institutions and the history of educational philosophy should not be treated as two separate histories. They are two mutually dependent elements within a unified history of theory and practice.

Finally, any coherent historical explanation of how and why the idea of education as intrinsically related to the development of reason originated and evolved will require an historical argument that unfolds through a number of historical stages. The first stage is that in which the ability to reason first emerged in prehistoric times to play a crucial part in the evolution of the human species and the emergence of the distinctive human activity we call 'education.' The second is that in which this activity became intrinsically related to the development of human reason. The third is that in which this understanding of education became embedded in the culture of Western societies and, as it progressed from one historical period to another, was revised to take account of changing cultural circumstances and new social conditions. The fourth is that in which a politicised conception of education emerged to pave the way for the rise of modern mass schooling: a system of education that that can only be defended in utilitarian terms.

What, then, will provide this history with its unity and coherence is that it is organised around episodes and events that constitute significant moments in a historical quest to advance the idea of education as the development of reason. It will give due recognition to those prominent philosophers who critically repudiated educational ideas and beliefs that were impeding the practical realisation of this quest and thereby transformed our understanding of how it should be pursued. But it will not be a history of inevitable progress. Instead, it will show how the pursuit of this quest has been fraught with difficulties and dangers and, at times, abandoned and disowned. It will also identify those occasions when it has been frustrated, resisted and opposed – not only passively, by the dead weight of history, but also explicitly and openly by the reactions of those whose interests it threatens. And it will conclude by showing how education today is embedded in a culture in which the idea of education as the development or reason has been systematically rejected and replaced.

A full-length history not only of the different ways that education has been practised and understood in the western world but also of the educational philosophies embodying these differences would fill several volumes. Moreover, a short history that starts with the origins of education and ends in our own modern times not only has to simplify, omit and select but also to compromise and compress. Adopting such a long-distance, wide-ranging historical perspective has made it necessary to extract information from a number of published books, scholarly journal articles, commentaries, websites and other secondary sources.

Like much else in this book, the view of education it adopts of the relationship between the history and the philosophy is not in any way original. My claim that the history of education is inherently philosophical simply endorses the view of the relationship between philosophy and history originally articulated by the 19th-century German philosopher Georg Wilhelm Friedrich Hegel (1770–1831) and subsequently advanced by eminent philosophers as different as R.G. Collingwood (1946), Hans-Georg Gadamer (1980) and Charles Taylor (1984). I also have to acknowledge that in writing this book I have enlisted the aid of a diverse range of authors who have little in common with each other but who each, in their own important way, proved to be invaluable in helping me to clarify my intentions and refine my understanding of what I was trying to achieve. Since this book owes so much to these authors, I feel obliged to give them full recognition.

First, the title of this book is a deliberate allusion to Max Horkheimer's seminal text *Eclipse of Reason* (1947) in which he examines how the concept of reason has been interpreted throughout the history of Western philosophy. For Horkheimer, as for many other 20th-century philosophers, the most disturbing feature of modern Western culture is the threat it poses to the future of human reason. He argues that, in modern societies, reason has been reduced to a mere instrument for achieving predetermined ends and that this has deprived individuals of their ability to rationally determine purposes and discover ends that can furnish sufficient reason for their activities and so render these activities reasonable and worthwhile. In many ways, my purpose in this book is to show how the cultivation of this ability to reason about the ends of human action became a defining aim of Western education and to expose the adverse consequences of its modern 'eclipse' for our understanding of education today.

Another philosophical text that considers the educational ramifications of the modern demise of human reason is Pádraig Hogan's *The Custody and Courtship of Experience: Western Education in Philosophical Perspective* (1995) which examines how major figures in the history of western philosophy have shaped the rise and decline of a distinctive conception of education that was initially formulated in classical antiquity. I have drawn extensively on Hogan's ideas and insights and the influence of his book cannot be overestimated. I also have to acknowledge the importance of Glen Langford's *Education, Persons and Society: A Philosophical Enquiry* (1985) in helping me to understand the important part played by educational philosophies in shaping the history of educational institutions and practices.

Finally, it would be no exaggeration to say that my book would not – and perhaps could not – have been written in the way that it has without my having read and re-read the work of one the foremost philosophers in the English-speaking world, Alasdair MacIntyre. Two of his books have been particularly influential. These are *A Short History of Ethics* (1967) in which he examines the relationship between moral philosophy and moral conduct from Ancient Greece to the present day; and his seminal text *After Virtue: A Study in Moral Theory* (1981) in which he constructs a compelling historical argument to show why we now live in a cultural milieu in which human behaviour can no longer governed by moral reasoning. It is by reading these two books that I have learned that the history of educational practice and the history of educational philosophy are one and the same. And it is by reading these books that I have been able to understand better how the conception of education whose history this book seeks to analyse and describe originated and evolved.

References

Collingwood, R.G. (1946) *The Idea of History*. Oxford: Oxford University Press.

Gadamer, H-G. (1980) *Truth and Method* (trans. G. Bardey and J. Cummings). New York: Seabury Press.

Hogan, P. (1995) '*The Custody and Courtship of Experience: Western Education in Philosophical Perspective*.'Dublin: Columba Press.

Horkheimer, M. (1947) *Eclipse of Reas*on. Oxford: Oxford University Press.

Langford, G. (1985) *Education, Persons and Society: A Philosophical Enquiry*. Basingstoke: Macmillan.

MacIntyre, A. C. (1967*) A Short History of Ethic*. London: Routledge and Kegan Paul Ltd.

MacIntyre, A. C. (1981) *After Virtue: A Study in Moral Theory*. London: Duckworth.

Taylor, C. (1984) 'Philosophy and Its History' in R. Rorty, J. B. Schneewind and Q. Skinner (eds) *Philosophy and History*. Cambridge: Cambridge University Press.

2 The Birth of Reason and the Origins of Education

Some two-and-a-half million years ago, in the forests of Africa, a new animal evolved from the hominid family of Great Apes that we now call *Homo*, the Latin word for 'man.' Some earlier species, such as *Homo habilis* and *Homo erectus*, migrated to Europe and Asia where they managed to survive for the best part of two million years. Over time, several other species evolved, all sharing a unique combination of physical traits that made them different from other primates: they had large brains; they could walk on two legs and so were able to work with their hands; and they had an opposable thumb, which allowed them to make and use stone tools. These physical attributes did not give our early ancestors any special advantages over other members of the animal kingdom. They were fairly weak creatures, occupying a position somewhere in the middle of the food chain, living in constant fear of lions, tigers and other predators.

As recently as 200,000 years ago, a new species appeared in east Africa: *Homo sapiens* – the species to which we all belong. Like other species, *Homo sapiens* lived as nomadic 'hunter-gatherers,' moving from place to place in a constant search for animals to hunt and plants to eat. About 150,000 years ago, they began to develop some new physical features: they acquired a more delicate skeleton and a more rounded skull; they had higher foreheads, a more pointed chin and a smaller face. In other words, they became 'anatomically modern' humans – the term now used to distinguish *homo sapiens* that are, physically, just like us.

About 70,000 years ago, these anatomically modern humans migrated from east Africa to Europe and Asia. Over the next 55,000 years all other human species –most notably *Homo*

DOI: 10.4324/9781003625735-2

neanderthalensis – began to disappear. About 13,000 years ago, only *Homo sapiens* remained. Why? What was the secret of our ancestors' success? Why did they survive while all other human species became extinct? The simple answer is that – between 70,000 and 30,000 years ago – our ancestors developed the ability to speak and think in unprecedented ways. The appearance of these new ways of thinking and communicating constitute what Yuval Noah Harari refers to as the "Cognitive Revolution' (Harari 2011, p. 23). It was – and will probably always remain – the most monumental event in human history.

Explanations of what caused this revolution are entirely speculative. One theory is that accidental genetic mutations changed the inner workings of the human brain in a way that enabled the species to communicate in a new kind of language. Like many other animals, *Homo sapiens* already had a limited vocal language which enabled them to talk to one another using various distinct call sounds. But now they were able to produce an infinite number of sentences that not only transformed their ability to communicate with each other, it also enhanced their ability to perform a whole range of new mental activities such as remembering, imagining, planning and calculating. Gradually, they acquired the capacity to reason which, in turn enabled them to think creatively and symbolically, reflect on their circumstances, discuss the merits of alternative courses of action and devise and carry out new and more complex survival strategies. About 50,000 years ago, these cognitive and behavioural developments led to the emergence of 'behaviourally modern' humans with the same intellectual, emotional and behavioural abilities as humans living today.

Although *Homo sapiens* were now able to collect, remember and share a huge amount of information about events occurring in the natural world, they did not know what caused them. They knew that floods, earthquakes and other natural catastrophise happened but had no idea why. To overcome this lack of understanding, they began to do something that no other animal can do: they created and shared mythical stories about an imaginary world that did not actually exist. In many of these stories, benevolent spirits, evil demons and other supernatural beings would symbolise the forces of good and evil in tales of extraordinary events that occurred at an unspecified time and in a place beyond the realms of human experience. And, by believing that these myths provided indubitable facts about the natural world, *Homo sapiens* could satisfy their need to answer questions that would otherwise remain beyond human comprehension.

As these stories became widely believed, they began to provide a set of shared beliefs that could bind otherwise isolated individuals together. This enabled them to forge a common identity, adopt a shared perception of the workings of the natural world and develop more sophisticated ways of communicating with each other. It also gave *Homo sapiens* the ability to act cooperatively in large numbers. To facilitate more effective forms of collective action, they began to live in closer proximity to each other and so adopt a more communal form of life. Whereas they had previously lived in small bands of 10–15 individuals, they now began to live in tribes with several hundred people living together in a more or less orderly community with the kind of enduring social groups and organised patterns of roles, rules and relationships that constitute what we now call a 'society.' As each society began to adopt its own myths, language, norms, rituals, customs and conventions, it began to adopt those distinctive attitudes, values and patterns of behaviour that constitute what we now call a 'culture.' And with the appearance of societies, each with its own cultural identity, *Homo sapiens* were no longer confined to living in the natural world. They now inhabited an imaginary – or, as sociologists would say, 'socially constructed' – reality that became possible only because of their unique ability to speak about, and believe in, a fictional reality that only existed in their collective imagination.

Because it is the product of the collective human imagination, a society could be sustained over time only if its social norms and cultural components could be passed from one generation to the next through the processes of 'socialisation' and 'enculturation.' For the most part, these processes occurred simultaneously and naturally through the everyday practices of nurturing or upbringing and involved little more than each new generation learning from the previous generation what they needed to know for their social and cultural life to be preserved. But as well as operating to maintain the social and cultural status quo, this process of intergenerational learning also made it possible for humans to transform their social and cultural life by the simple expedient of transmitting different myths and telling different stories. This ability to change the social and cultural environment was to have profound consequences for the subsequent development of the human species. For more than two million years the parameters of human behaviour had been biologically fixed and changed slowly over hundreds of thousands of years. Now the process of intergenerational learning made it possible for humans to transmit a host of new behaviours to the next generation quickly, without any need for genetic mutations or evolutionary change. Gradually, the slow process of biological evolution and change was superseded by the rapid process of social and cultural evolution and change. Narrative accounts of the complexities surrounding the most significant periods of social and cultural change are what we call 'history.'

While prior to the Cognitive Revolution *Homo sapiens* could only react passively to their natural environment, they could now respond positively to the exigencies of nature, shaping and controlling it to their own wishes and demands. It is therefore unsurprising that the revolution in *Homo sapiens*' cognitive and linguistic abilities led to an unprecedented array of achievements. These included the invention of more sophisticated and specialised tools such as fishhooks, harpoons, darts. oil lamps, bows and arrows and needles (Harari 2011, p. 23). Also, the 50,000-year period following the Cognitive Revolution was, by all accounts, a 'golden age.' The life of *Homo sapiens* was comfortable, egalitarian and peaceful. Food was plentiful; there were no social hierarchies, no private property and no wars. Nobody was concerned about their own personal wealth, social status or political power. There were no nuclear families or monogamous relationships and all adults cooperated in the upbringing of each other's children. Initially, this simply involved everyday child-rearing practices that were not differentiated from other social and cultural activities. But as *Homo sapiens* began to recognise how modifying and revising the content and form of these practices could bring about social and cultural improvements, questions about what should be learned by the next generation became subject to sophisticated human reflection. Over time, as these questions began to be more systematically and explicitly addressed, natural child-rearing practices were gradually assimilated into a more self-consciously performed and more culturally defined set of social practices that became divorced from everyday life and incorporated into a more formalised and culturally regulated human activity: education.

So, education first emerged towards the later stages of the Palaeolithic age as an attempt to intervene in the natural processes of child-rearing and socialisation. Needless to say, the kind of education that existed during this period did not require teachers or anything remotely resembling a school. However, once the interrelationship between social change and educational change became obvious, individuals and social groups began to routinely assess whether the education being provided to the rising generation should be changed to meet the needs of their community more effectively. Although there is no way of knowing how this evaluative process would have occurred, this did not prevent J. Abner Peddiwell – an American professor of the history of education – from writing his famous satirical text *The Saber-Tooth Curriculum*, (2004) in which he tells a fictional story of how about 11,000 years ago, a tribe changed its curriculum in order to overcome numerous survival problems caused by the ending of the last Ice Age.

Peddiwell's story begins by describing how education in a Palaeolithic tribe was based on a curriculum that had initially been introduced to improve the kind of knowledge and skills being taught to the younger generation in order to ensure that they could have better food, shelter and protection than previous generations. This curriculum – the Saber-Tooth Curriculum – was made up of three core subjects: 'fish-grabbing-with-bare-hands'; 'woolly-horse-clubbing'; and 'saber-tooth-scaring-with-fire.' But, as the Ice Age grew to a close, a massive glacier began to melt, polluting the rivers and streams where the tribe caught fish. Soon the water became so muddy that it was no longer possible to see any fish to catch. The melting glacier had also turned the banks of the rivers into boggy marshes and the woolly horses that had always gone to the river for water migrated to the dry open plains. As they moved away, they were replaced in the tribe's traditional hunting ground by herds of small antelopes that moved so quickly that nobody could get close enough to club them. Another consequence of the melting glacier was that the climate became damper and more humid, resulting in large numbers of sabre-tooth tigers dying from pneumonia. Soon there were no sabretooth tigers to scare. Instead, tribal security now faced a new threat: the arrival of ferocious glacial bears that could not be driven away by the traditional 'scaring-with-fire' techniques.

In these circumstances it quickly became obvious that the knowledge and skills learned in the Saber-Tooth Curriculum had become obsolete. One member of the tribe, recognising how environmental changes had created new survival problems, came up with the novel idea of catching fish by submerging nets made from tree vines into the muddy water of the river. When his idea was put into practice the results were so positive that the tribe now had more fish than it ever had using the 'fish-grabbing-with-bare-hands' technique. Another member of the tribe, realising that the 'woolly-horse-clubbing' technique was useless for catching the elusive antelopes, bent a young tree over an antelope trail and fixed it with a noosed vine in such a way that the passing animal would be snared when the tree jerked upright. This proved to be so successful that he was able to secure more meat and skins in one night than a dozen horse-clobbers had been able to secure in a week. A third tribesman, alarmed by how the newly arrived glacial bears posed a serious threat to the tribe's safety, decided to dig a deep pit across a bear trail and cover it with branches. He then waited to see if the bears would fall into the pit and remain trapped until they could be killed. The positive results result of his experiment meant that the tribe not only had more security than before but also a new source of meat and skins. Soon everyone recognised that that the tribe could only survive if the core subjects of the *Saber- Tooth Curriculum* were replaced by the more relevant subjects of 'fish-net-making,' 'snare-setting' and 'bear-pit-digging.'

Abner Pediwell's story paints a fictional, but an entirely plausible, picture of how, towards the end of the Palaeolithic period, *Homo sapiens* might have changed their existing educational arrangements in order to meet their survival needs at times of social change. And, as this process of educational change gradually enabled *Homo sapiens* to develop more advanced methods for meeting their survival needs, they eventually reached the stage when it became possible to abandon the nomadic life of the hunter-gatherer and instead adopt a different way of life that was to dramatically revolutionise how humans lived. So, about 10,000 years ago, began the first Agricultural Revolution.

The transition from a life of hunting and gathering to one of farming and agriculture began with the cultivation of plants and the domestication of animals. The first plants to be cultivated were wheat, rice and corn. The first animals to be domesticated were horses, dogs, oxen, goats and sheep. People stopped moving from place to place and instead began to live in permanent villages, usually located in areas with arable land. Gradually, these tribal villages began to gravitate towards regions where rivers made the land more fertile and productive. About 8,000 years ago, numerous villages sprung up across the area between the rivers Tigris and Euphrates that the Greeks were later to call Mesopotamia – literally 'the land between two rivers.' These villages were rural, communal and egalitarian. They practised small-scale subsistence farming, with individuals living and working collectively in small communities made up of their immediate kinship groups. About 6,000 years ago, several villages decided that their lives would be improved if they lived and worked together in one large permanent settlement. The result was the creation of the first city –Uruk – some 250 kilometres south of Bagdad. Over the next 3,000 years, many more Mesopotamian villages joined together to form cities with communities much larger and more complex than their immediate kinship groups. By 2500 BC, 80 percent of the population of Mesopotamia lived in cities, each with a population of between 15,000 and 30,000 (Miles 2010, pp. 3–4).

Because of their concentrated populations, cities could supply the large workforce needed to construct complex irrigation systems based on an elaborate system of dams and canals. This intensified the pace of technological development: new tools were invented; new irrigation methods were devised; and more sophisticated farming techniques were developed. This led to the production of large food surpluses which could sustain workers in industries such as weaving, leatherwork, masonry, pottery and building. With the emergence of specialist workers, new social identities were formed and new occupational roles created. By 2,500 BC the small, egalitarian tribal villages that had originally settled in Mesopotamia had all but been replaced by urban cities with power concentrated in the hands of a ruling elite who controlled food production, levied and collected taxes and upheld law and order. The customs and conventions that had governed the tribal way of life were discarded in favour of a centralised system of codified laws which allowed the many to be controlled by the few. And an egalitarian way of life was replaced by an elitist system of social relations which consigned many to the position of labourers and slaves. These feature of Mesopotamian cities – urbanisation, centralisation, social stratification, the division of labour and a social hierarchy with a ruling elite – were, and still remain, the defining characteristics of the unique form of social order we call 'civilisation.'

Mesopotamian cities could only sustain this new social order if tens of thousands of their inhabitants were prepared to accept a life of misery and poverty and occupy social roles that denied them any access to positions of wealth, status or power. This seemingly impossible task was accomplished by conjuring up stories that featured a new kind of mythical creature: gods. The inhabitants of early tribal villages had religious beliefs but never in their wildest dreams would they have imagined that there existed some supernatural entities that had to be worshipped and obeyed. Still less did they have anything remotely resembling an organised religion. But Mesopotamians created dozens of gods who between them had power over every conceivable aspect of human existence. Prominent amongst these were Enki, the god of water and the creator of humankind; Enili, the god who had initially separated heaven from earth; and An, the god of the sky, the ruler of heaven and the source of all earthly power and authority.

These Mesopotamian gods were the main characters in a number of fictional stories that the inhabitants of Mesopotamian cities believed offered incontrovertible truths about how the natural world was created, the meaning of human existence and, crucially, why different individuals were destined to live different lives. Once these beliefs could be ingrained into the collective consciousness of a city's inhabitants, they created a common unifying bond between thousands of unrelated individuals and so provided the cement holding together a social order in which the relationships between unequal social groups that would otherwise be hostile, antagonistic and acrimonious could be rendered cooperative and harmonious. It is not for nothing that, 4,000 years later, Karl Marx was to describe religion as the opium of the masses.

A collective belief in these religious myths also legitimised theocracy: a form of government in which political power was firmly in the hands of a small elite made up of those self-appointed gatekeepers to the gods: priests. As both the representatives of the gods and the mediators between the gods and the people, Mesopotamian priests were invested with divine authority to impose and collect taxes, make and enforce laws and generally control all aspects of people's lives. But their most important role was to inculcate the theocracy's prescribed myths, dogmas and doctrines with a severity sufficient to ensure that they were blindly accepted as true. Initially, these dogmas and doctrines could only be transmitted orally and so could only be conserved in the collective consciousness of a single generation. But, sometime between 3100 BC and 3400 BC, Mesopotamian civilisation found a way of overcoming this problem: the invention of writing. With the advent of writing, religious myths and legends that might otherwise have been lost and forgotten could now be preserved as sacred texts to be taught and learned as the depository of received wisdom and eternal truth.

The earliest writing system to emerge in Mesopotamia was pictography, which involved inscribing pictures representing objects into soft clay tablets. By 3500 BC pictography had evolved into a form of writing known as cuneiform, which involved pressing a writing implement, known as a *stylus*, into clay, to produce wedge-like impressions representing something like modern-day words. Originally writing was used to make lists of people, places and things but, within a few hundred years, cuneiform tablets were being baked hard enough to provide permanent records of business transactions, legal documents, farming inventories and financial accounts. By 2000 BC more or less everything was being written down: laws were codified; medical cures were documented; and the most mundane details of urban life were recorded.

Prior to the invention of writing, Mesopotamian children would pick up what they needed to know and learn from parents, priests and other adults. Boys would be taught how to farm by farmers; girls would be taught how to cook, clean and sew by their mothers; and priests would initiate the young into religious myths, rites and rituals and give sermons about how to avoid the wrath of the gods. But teaching children how to write was different. Cuneiform was a complex skill that that could only be learned over a long period of time, in an institution dedicated to this purpose, from those who had already mastered it. So, for the first time, there appeared a new group of professional experts – teachers – working in institutions that were exclusively concerned with teaching and learning – schools.

The first Mesopotamian schools were called *eduba* – literally 'scribal school'– and were usually located in the city temple. The teachers in early Mesopotamian schools were scribes whose main method of teaching was to write a sentence on a clay tablet and then get their students to copy it repeatedly until they could write it without any errors. Mistakes were punished by severe beating. The school-day lasted from dawn to dusk. Students started school when they were seven or eight and stayed until they were nineteen years old. Over time, schools began to teach other subjects such as geography, zoology, botany, astronomy, engineering, medicine and architecture. Tuition was costly, so a formal education was only available to boys of wealthy families. After they left school, students would become priests, scribes or senior government officials.

Mesopotamian scribal schools marked the transformation of education from a human activity primarily concerned with meeting survival needs into a formal institution that played a key role in maintaining the political and religious culture of Mesopotamian society. In doing this, it introduced many of the practices that were to characterise education for many centuries to come. These include methods of teaching that relied on memorisation and rote learning; the routine use of corporal punishment; and the restriction of education to a privileged male elite.

As well as creating the first system of formal schooling, Mesopotamia is also credited with the invention of the wheel which, together with the invention of the wooden sailboat, provided the means of land and sea transportation needed to expand travel and trade. By 3000 BC trade routes running from Mesopotamia to the eastern Mediterranean had made it possible for people from different places to travel back and forth, so facilitating the exchange of ideas, knowledge and cultures. Slowly but surely, the influence of Mesopotamian civilisation began to spread. Several Phoenician cities grew up in what is now Lebanon and Syria, each with the social, cultural, political and economic features of a civilisation.

Around 2000 BC, the first civilisation in the western Mediterranean – the Minoan civilisation – emerged in Crete, only to be superseded quickly by the Mycenaean civilisation – the first advanced civilisation to be established on mainland Greece – which itself collapsed in about 1100 BC. Roughly three centuries later, the Greeks modified the existing Phoenician alphabet to include five new letters to represent vowels, so making it possible to write literature in the form of poetic prose. In the eighth century BC, the Greek poet Homer used this new literary genre to write his famous epic poems. So began what is conventionally known as 'Classical Antiquity,' a period that lasted until the fall of the Roman Empire in the fifth century AD. It was a period of unprecedented cultural and political achievements from which Western civilisation was to derive many of its ideas and ideals in areas as diverse as politics, art, architecture, law, philosophy and poetry. And it was during this period that the foundations were laid for the distinctive understanding of education in terms of which all significant episodes and events in the subsequent history of Western education came to be identified, evaluated and understood.

References

Harari, Y. N (2011) *Sapiens: A Brief History of Humankind*. London: Penguin.

Miles, R. (2010) *Ancient Worlds: The Search for the Origins of Western Civilizations*. London: Penguin.

Peddiwell, J. Abner. (2004) *The Saber-Tooth Curriculum*. Maidenhead: McGraw-Hill.

3 Antiquity

The Formation of the Western Educational Tradition

About 800 BC a number of Greek tribal villages began to develop into independent city states, each with its own political, judicial, legal and religious institutions and each located in a large centrally located open space known as the *agora.* Despite their differences, all these city states – or, as they were known, *poleis* – shared some common features. They all spoke the same language and had the same customs and religion; they all had some sort of constitution, raised armies, collected taxes and passed laws. But their most important common characteristic was a distinctive understanding of what it was to be 'Greek' that allowed their inhabitants to forge a common cultural identity that differentiated them from the uncivilised non-Greeks who they disparagingly dismissed as 'barbarians'.

This identity had its roots in the stories told by Homer in his famous epic poems: *The Iliad* (2003a), which recounts battles and events during the ten-year siege of the city of Troy; and *The Odyssey* (2003b), that depicts the perils and adventures of Odysseus during his long journey home from the Trojan war. They describe the super-human feats of heroic figures such as Achilles and Hercules, and their relationship to a pantheon of divine deities such as Zeus, Apollo and Aphrodite. And, as with all mythical stories, they provided beliefs and explanations that laid the foundations for the formation of the Greeks' understanding of themselves and their social and cultural world.

However, in the seventh century BC a group of Greek intellectuals began to wonder whether basing their beliefs about themselves and their world on myths was simplistic and naïve. The founder of this group – Thales of Miletus (624–548 BC), – was a mathematician and astronomer who thought that the world would be better understood

DOI: 10.4324/9781003625735-3

by explanations that rested solely on careful observations, systematic reasoning and a disinterested search for the truth. Initially this group became part of what was to become known as 'the Ionian School': a collection of thinkers who conducted intellectual inquiries using nothing other than a systematic appeal to human reason. Towards the end of the sixth century, Pythagoras of Samos (547–495 BC) designated this mode of intellectual activity *philosophia*, literally a love of wisdom. The term *philos*, the Greek word for 'love', designated the disposition of a person whose life was totally devoted to a particular activity, while *sophia* covered a range of rational virtues that together constituted 'wisdom'. *Philosophia* therefore bore little resemblance to a modern academic discipline. It simply referred to the way of life adopted by those devoted to pursuing a rational understanding of culture, science, religion, politics, reality and human existence.

By the fifth century BC, intellectuals committed to a philosophical way of life could be found in most Greek city states. But one city state that positively disparaged any kind of serious intellectual activity was Sparta, a warrior society that reached the height of its power after defeating Athens in the Peloponnesian War (431–404 BC). Sparta's overriding preoccupation was with protecting itself from the ever-present danger of war. In their vigorous pursuit of this objective, the Spartans created a formal education system devoted to a single purpose: turning all male citizens into highly trained solders with the physical strength and the military skill to defend their *polis*. This programme, known as the *agoge* (roughly translated as 'rearing') was built on the principles of excruciating austerity, obsessional physical fitness and unquestioning loyalty to the Spartan state.

The *agoge* was divided into three stages. The first began at the age of seven when boys were removed from the custody of their parents and sent to live in a barracks. In an effort to force them to learn how to forage, steal and endure acute hunger and extreme pain – qualities that were regarded as necessary during a war – they were given little food and subject to harsh discipline. The second stage began at the age of 12 and was designed to further enhance strength and endurance through intense physical training and even harsher discipline. When they were 17, students entered the third stage of the *agoge*, during which they competed in gymnastics and took part in planned battles with real weapons. After two years, they officially became Spartan soldiers. Somewhat surprisingly young girls also received a formal education, supervised and controlled by the state. Its main purpose was to train them for their primary task: to give birth to fit and healthy males for the Spartan army. They were taught dance, gymnastics and other sports, together with subjects such as music and poetry and writing. However, traits such as grace and culture were frowned upon in favour of high physical fitness and moral integrity.

Although Spartan education is often dismissed as little more than a full-time military training camp, it was the first state-provided compulsory education system that was available to all rather than being restricted to a privileged elite. However, in Ancient Greece, Spartan education was the exception rather than the rule. Most other city states adopted a system of education known as *paideia*: a form of education designed to equip people to participate in the life of the *polis*. For the Greeks, the overriding concern of *paideia* was with the transmission and acquisition of *arête*, which is often translated as 'virtue' but is better translated as 'human excellence' or 'perfection'. *Arête* was a central ideal of Greek culture and was first used to describe the moral virtues – physical strength, courage, honour, duty and the like – possessed by the heroes who filled the pages of the *Iliad* and the *Odyssey,* but later came to include intellectual virtues such as honesty, truthfulness and wisdom. Those individuals who had been educated to pursue *arête* – those who strived for perfection – were designated the *aristoi*, literally 'the best'. For the Greeks, it was only the *aristoi* who could excel in performing their political and social roles and it was only an education in *arete* that would guarantee that the *polis* was governed by an *aristokratia*, literally 'rule by the best'.

The city state where education was most firmly entrenched in *paideia* was Athens. Unlike Spartan education, it was private rather than public and elitist rather than egalitarian. Schools were small, with a single teacher teaching a range of subjects that included gymnastics, grammar rhetoric, music, mathematics, geography, natural history and philosophy. They were expensive, with access limited to children of the wealthy aristocratic families who could afford to pay their fees. Formal education was divided into three distinct stages: primary, secondary and tertiary. Primary education started at age seven and focused on writing, reading, arithmetic, music and Homer's epic poems. The secondary stage began at age 14 and focused on rhetoric, grammar and philosophy as well as subjects such as science history, geography, biology and chemistry. The tertiary stage was concerned with physical fitness, with students practising wrestling, jumping, running, gymnastics and athletics. After completing their formal education able-bodied young men had to undertake two years of military training. By then they would be able to take their place as members of the *aristokratia* whose education had made them the 'best' people to govern.

Prior to the seventh century BC, the Athenian *polis* was controlled by an *oligarkhia* – rule by the few – in which political power was confined to a small number of people chosen from the *aristoi.* But in 508 BC Athens replaced this aristocratic oligarchy with *demokratia* – 'rule by the people' – a form of government based on the radical idea that all citizens should govern and rule themselves. However, Athenians did not regard democracy simply as a system for electing political leaders. Rather, its primary virtue was that it created a form of communal life in which all citizens were able to realise their distinctively human capacities by collectively participating in rational discussions about how to pursue their common good. In this sense, Athenian democracy embodied an educational ideal: to educate all people to the point where their intellectual, social and moral capacities have reached their full potential, and they are able to participate freely and equally in the life of their community.

Although democracy meant 'rule by the people' only adult Athenian citizens – about 10% of the population – were classified as 'the people'. Women, children and foreigners were excluded as, of course, were all barbarians and slaves. Also, because most Athenians who qualified as citizens had to work for a living, the wealthy *aristokratia* continued to hold most of the major offices of state and maintain control of the *polis*. The only difference was that they were now democratically accountable and so needed to justify their political decisions, argue their case and persuade other Athenian citizens to accept their arguments. Prior to the emergence of democracy, it was assumed that it was sufficient for aspiring politicians to have been educated to pursue *arête* by means of *paideia.* But now they also had to learn the oratorial skills needed to persuade their fellow citizens to accept their arguments and agree with their views. This need was more than met by the Sophists – literally 'wise men' – a group of mostly foreign itinerant teachers and philosophers who, in return for a fee, promised to teach young Athenian aristocrats how to succeed in political life. As teachers, they taught the art of rhetoric – the art of appealing to people's irrational prejudices with the sole purpose of gaining support and access to the levers of political power. As philosophers, they argued that there are no rational criteria for judging the truth of political beliefs and that the only thing politicians needed to know was how to use the techniques of rhetorical persuasion to seduce an audience into accepting a particular point of view. But at the same time as the Sophists were offering anyone with the time and money a form of higher education whose only aim was political success, there appeared a travelling teacher who did not charge fees, was deeply suspicious of the Sophists' teachings and presented a radically different view of how young Athenians should be educated: the enigmatic philosopher Socrates (470–399 BC).

Like other Greek philosophers, Socrates saw himself as a 'lover of wisdom', pursuing true knowledge solely through the use of human reason. He also shared his predecessors' conviction that questions about the world could not be adequately answered by resorting to the traditional stories and myths that lay at the heart of Greek culture but should be based on nothing other than a systematic appeal to human reason and a disinterested search for the truth. But Socrates differed from all previous philosophers in two important respects. First, while they were primarily concerned with theoretical questions about such matters as the nature of reality and the origins of the universe, Socrates was preoccupied with practical questions concerning the right way to live. Second, while other philosophers claimed to use the power of reason to discover true knowledge, he insisted that they actually knew nothing. For Socrates, the only thing that made philosophers different from everyone else was that they were consciously aware of their own ignorance, an insight encapsulated in the famous Socratic paradox 'the only thing I know is that I know nothing'.

Although he insisted that his own ignorance prevented him from teaching his students anything, this did not prevent him from teaching his students to understand how to live a life that is morally desirable and personally fulfilling. But if this understanding could not be taught through instruction, how was it to be acquired? Socrates' answer was that individuals had to acquire it for themselves through a process of critical self-reflection. To facilitate this process, he devised a method of teaching that was strikingly different from anything that had gone before and was forever to become known as the 'Socratic method'.

Unlike other teaching methods, Socrates' method was not designed to transmit a body of authoritative knowledge. It simply involved engaging his students in a type of rational dialogue that the Greeks called 'dialectic': a discussion between two or more people whose only concern was to discover the truth. To this end, Socrates would ask his students questions designed to expose the assumptions implicit in their understanding of how they ought to live their lives. He would then invite them to rationally examine these assumptions in order to assess their truth. This invariably revealed that their answers to his initial question relied on beliefs they had uncritically absorbed from Greek culture and tradition. Socrates would then ask further questions designed to reveal how these beliefs are erroneous or contradictory and so force his students to admit that they lack any rational justification. But, of course, he never actually tried to provide his students with true answers to his initial question. Rather, the whole purpose of his teaching method was to make them critically question their inherited ways of thinking and thereby question what they previously thought they knew. Through this process of self-critical questioning, Socrates' students would begin to recognise any rational inadequacies in their thinking and so acquire the kind of reflective self-knowledge that would allow them to reconsider whether what they believed was rationally justifiable and question the values and assumptions that guided their lives. For Socrates, then, the good teacher is someone who has the insight, skills and judgement to initiate the process of dialectical questioning that would lead their students to discover the kind of self-knowledge that, for Socrates, was the source of all wisdom.

Since Socrates' overriding purpose was to force young Athenian citizens to answer critical questions about their conventional beliefs, they started to realise that many of these rested on contrived rationalisations designed to legitimise the political status quo. As a result, they began to confront their political leaders with some awkward questions and subject their answers to the kind of critical scrutiny that the Socratic method required. It goes without saying that teaching the young how to expose the rational inadequacy of conventional moral and political thinking hardly endeared Socrates to the Athenian political elite. It is a mark of his success that the political authorities found it necessary to accuse him of corrupting the youth of Athens, a charge for which he was found guilty and sentenced to death.

Socrates' contribution to the history of education is often taken to be his invention of a method of teaching. But his most important and enduring historical legacy is a vision of what education is which he never explicitly articulated but to which he always implicitly subscribed. What his teaching method presupposed and required was a commitment to a form of education that does not simply serve the social, political or economic needs of society, offers no social advantages or material rewards and benefits nobody but those who receive it. Its essential purpose is to enable learners to engage in an unimpeded and unending search for the truth in order to expose and rationally reassess the inherited cultural, moral, political and religious beliefs that shaped their understanding of themselves and how they should live. To the extent that it enables learners to become self-consciously aware of their own hitherto unquestioned beliefs, it obeys Socrates' injunction 'Know thyself!' And to the extent that it requires them to critically examine their understanding of themselves, it gives expression to Socrates' famous assertion 'the unexamined life is not worth living'.

Socrates would have ridiculed the suggestion that he had anything remotely resembling an educational philosophy. Also, since he never actually wrote anything, he is known mainly through the 35 *Socratic Dialogues* written by his dedicated and most famous student, Plato (428–348 BC). Although Plato's aristocratic background made politics his obvious career, two important events led him to decide otherwise. The first was the Peloponnesian Wars (460–404 BC) which ended in defeat for Athens and led to the temporary replacement of democracy by tyranny. Plato puts much of the blame for Athens' defeat on its democratic form of government which, by privileging equality over *arête,* denied the right to rule to the *aristoi* who, by virtue of their education and superior intelligence, were best equipped to do so. This hostility was reinforced by the execution of Socrates, which he saw as a gross abuse of power by democratically elected politicians who lacked the intellectual capacity and moral integrity needed to exercise political authority. Disgusted by Socrates' execution, Plato turned his back on public life and, in 387 BC, founded *The Academy*, a philosophy school that prepared aspiring statesmen to become leading members of the Athenian *polis*. Eight years later, Plato set out the details of an 'academic' education in his most famous Socratic dialogue: *The Republic* (Plato, 1974). Like virtually all of Plato's works, *The Republic* is written as a dialogue in which Socrates uses his dialectical method to ask prominent Greek Sophists questions about the form of government that would best serve the common good. But as well as critically refuting their responses, Socrates is also made to provide answers that Plato believed to be valid and true. Because providing such answers is a very un-Socratic thing to do, it is highly likely that the Socrates portrayed in *The Republic* is simply a convenient mouthpiece for Plato's own, very different ideas.

The Republic offers a philosophical rationale for Plato's utopian vision of the ideal *polis*. It opens with Socrates asserting that any state can only meet its basic needs if it has three classes of citizens: workers to produce food and other material goods; soldiers to defend the state against its external enemies; and rulers to provide good administration and government. He then simply asserts that individuals are not all born the same: some are, by their very nature, driven by their basic desires and animal instincts; others are naturally courageous and brave; yet others have an innate ability to think and act in a predominantly rational way. From this he draws an obvious conclusion: that those in the first group are best suited to being workers; those in the second will make the best soldiers; those in the third, the best rulers. He further concludes that, since, the best life for any individual is a life doing what they are, by nature, predestined to do, and since the best state is one that effectively meets its material, military and administrative needs, the ideal state is one that imposes a rigid division of labour so as to achieve a harmonious correspondence between individuals and their predetermined social and occupational roles. In Plato's ideal state, the common good is best served by everyone knowing their place.

Given this view, the whole point of the educational system outlined in *The Republic* is to identify individuals in terms of their natural aptitudes and abilities and educate them for their appropriate social roles. To this end, Plato constructs a four-stage education programme based on Greek *paideia*. The first stage involves learning basic reading and writing skills, together with the inculcation of socially approved moral values and political beliefs. The second stage is a period of military training while the third involves study of maths, science and other theoretical subjects. The third stage is, in effect, a systematic study of philosophy. Individuals are only allowed to follow this educational programme as far as their natural ability permits and at the end of each stage there is a rigorous system of testing and selection designed to identify those who should be allowed to continue. For those destined for the labouring class education ends at the first stage and is replaced by vocational training, while the education of those destined to become soldiers terminates at stage two. Only the select few who have successfully completed all three stages are qualified to proceed to the fourth stage by following the education programme of the Academy; a rigorous 15-year programme of higher education that trains future leaders to become philosophers.

This training is primarily in dialectic, the art of conducting rational argument through the process of questioning and answering as exemplified by the Socratic method. But while Socrates insisted that the only kind of knowledge that dialectic produces is self-knowledge, Plato saw it as culminating in an abstract contemplation of the foundation of all true knowledge encapsulated in what he called the 'the Good'. He further contended that since only the philosophically educated can apprehend 'the Good', they alone can are fit to govern. In Plato's ideal state, philosophers rule or, as he famously concluded, 'It is only when philosophers are kings that ... our ideal state will see the light of day' (Plato, 1974, p.434).

While *The Republic* describes the education of an intellectual elite, *The Laws* – Plato's last, longest and perhaps most detested work – outlines the education appropriate for the children destined for the labouring classes (Plato, 2012). Since they inherently lacked the capacity for rational thought, Plato recommended that their education should focus on inculcating an unquestioning acceptance of their inferior social position by inducing a belief in all powerful gods, in particular the belief that to be obedient to the law is to be obedient before the gods. Plato also suggests that telling children stories at a very early age is an important pedagogical tool for the formation of their moral character. In particular, fables, myths and legends should be used to inculcate ideas and beliefs at an age when they are more likely to become indelibly fixed.

Just as Plato had been influenced by Socrates, so Plato had a decisive influence on Aristotle who was his student and colleague at the Academy for almost 20 years. Although there are many similarities between their philosophies, Aristotle thought that the educational programme outlined in Plato's *Republic* was far too abstract and elitist. For Aristotle the purpose of education was not to prepare an intellectually gifted elite to become political leader; it was simply to equip people to live the kind of life that they themselves actually desired. In the *Nicomachian Ethics* (1955) – the most brilliant set of lecture notes ever written – he pointed out what he regarded as an obvious truth: that what people desire is happiness. However, by 'happiness' he did not mean the transient experience of pleasure. The Greek word for happiness was *eudaimonia,* which is best understood as 'living well' or 'living a life that is good'. Aristotle took it to be a biological fact that what all animals most desire is to live in accordance with their own unique nature. And, since 'man' – though not 'woman' – was, by his very nature, a 'rational animal', it is only by realising his potential to reason that he can achieve *eudaimonia.*

For Aristotle, as for Plato, then, the purpose of education was to develop the human capacity to reason. However, unlike Plato, Aristotle did not think that this simply entailed developing the kind of theoretical reason that was developed through the philosophical education taught in the Academy. That type of reasoning – *episteme* – produces abstract theoretical knowledge of 'the Good' and is pursued in isolation from the practical concerns of everyday life. But, as Aristotle pointed out, attaining philosophical knowledge of the Good is not the same as knowing how to actually *do* what is good. Initially, this kind of knowledge is learned at an early age through a process of 'habituation' – a learning process that involves children constantly and repeatedly practising morally desirable behaviour until they habitually act in accordance with virtues such as honesty, courage, integrity, generosity and compassion. But while habituation is a necessary feature of a child's moral education, it is not sufficient. What is also required is the development of a form of reason that the Greeks called *phronesis* – practical reason – the form of reasoning used when choosing between competing, and perhaps conflicting, alternative options about what, in some concrete practical situation, would be the right thing to do. Aristotle insisted that *phronesis* is very different from *episteme.* It is not a methodical, rule-governed form of reasoning that can be taught and learned. It can only be cultivated through the accumulated experience of reflecting rationally on the morally relevant features of specific practical situations and, on this basis, making an informed decision about what ought to be done. Aristotle regarded *phronesis* as the supreme moral and intellectual virtue. Without it, moral judgement degenerated into intellectual calculation and becomes indistinguishable from mere cleverness. What distinguished those with a capacity for practical reasoning – the *phronimos* – is that they are able to see the particularities of a practical situation in the light of its ethical significance and act consistently on this basis. In other words, the *phronimos* are those who have been educated to do the right thing, in the right place, at the right time, in the right way.

Because of his stress on the educational importance of practical reason and moral development, Aristotle's version of *paideia* included subjects like music, gymnastics and drawing that he believed would both foster the process of habituation and help to cultivate the virtue of *phronesis*. His practical proposals are outlined in Book VIII of *Politics* (1986) and cover three distinct stages. The first stage for those aged 7–14 consisted of gymnastics, writing, reading, music and drawing. The second stage for those aged 14–21 continued their primary studies while adding literature, poetry, drama and dancing. The last four years would be spent in military drills, tactics and strategy. The third stage would begin at age 21 and provide a form of higher education that would continue as long as the student was willing and able.

The philosophies of Socrates, Plato and Aristotle were closely related. Plato saw himself as Socrates' successor, preserving and extending his teacher's legacy. Aristotle saw himself as Plato's heir, correcting the weaknesses and limitations of his predecessor's philosophical thought. Just as Plato agreed with many of Socrates' educational ideas but disagreed with others, so Aristotle sometimes agreed, and at other times disagreed, with Plato. One of their most important disagreements concerned their attitude to the education of women. Both Socrates and Plato were open to the idea of gender equality and refuted any suggestion that women should be denied equal access to the kind of education made available to men. Aristotle, on the other hand, held deep-seated misogynistic views, asserting that women were, by nature, intellectually and physically inferior and, for this reason, could not benefit from the sort of education suitable for men.

But, despite their differences, Socrates, Plato and Aristotle agreed that the unique and peculiar aim of education was to develop what they all believed to be essential to the achievement of *eudaimonia*: the ability to reason. Socrates emphasised the educational importance of critical reasoning, Plato gave pride of place to theoretical reasoning and Aristotle stressed the relevance of practical reasoning. But these differences should not obscure the fact that they all believed that the overriding purpose of education was to transform individuals who are initially nothing more than biological animals into civilised human beings able to think and act in a rational way. And it is this shared understanding of education that was to provide the point and purpose of a pattern of educational thought and action that has been conveyed across many generations through what we now call 'the Western educational tradition'.

Throughout its history, this tradition has been kept alive through an historically continuous argument about how the view of education on which it was erected ought to be practised and understood. The most important and influential participants in this argument have been those later European philosophers who, recognising that the arguments of Socrates, Plato and Aristotle were originally at home in a historical and cultural context that has long since disappeared, constructed their own arguments about how the distinctive understanding of education embedded in the tradition should be reinterpreted to take account of their own very different cultural and social milieu. And it is through this continuous process of critical reconstruction that later Western societies have been able to transcend the inadequacies and limitations of what had previously been thought, said and done within the tradition and so ensure that it would continue to progress and evolve rather than stagnate and decay.

Some of the philosophers participating in this process invoked the arguments of Plato; others agreed with Aristotle; yet others were inspired by the educational ideals of Socrates. But there is no doubt that the most influential representative of the Western educational tradition is Plato. The 20th-century philosopher Alfred North Whitehead is reputed to have said that the European philosophical tradition consists of a series of footnotes to Plato. This may or may not be true, but it is difficult to envisage Plato's views about education being totally abandoned without the Western educational tradition being virtually discarded. This, of course, does not mean that the continuity of the tradition has depended on disagreements over Plato's educational ideas and beliefs being avoided. Rather it is due to how these ideas became ingrained in the collective consciousness of Western civilisation and served to legitimise a social order in which it was assumed that individuals were 'by nature' unequal and education should be the preserve of an intellectual elite. Just as Mesopotamian mythology had provided a religious legitimation for a theocracy ruled by priests, so Plato's *Republic* offered a rationale for an aristocratic state ruled by philosophers. And just as Mesopotamian religious myths legitimised educational practices and institutions that sustained Mesopotamian civilisation for some 3,000 years, so Plato's *Republic* provided the canonical text for a tradition that has shaped the history of Western education until our own modern times.

One of the reasons why Plato's *Republic* was able to gain such prominence was the Roman conquest of Greece in 27 BC. Despite being conquered, virtually all aspects of classical Greek culture – philosophy, politics, mythology, religion, science and art – were integrated into Roman culture. So, when Rome began to set up a formal educational system, it adopted a version of Greek *paideia* that was heavily Romanised by the educational thinking of the rhetorician Marcus Fabius Quintilianus (35–100 AD) and the statesman and lawyer Marcus Tullius Cicero (106–43 BC), both of whom were influenced by Plato's *Republic.* Although Quintilian thought that Roman education should be primarily concerned with the cultivation of the orator, he also believed that future politicians needed to be well versed in Greek literature and philosophy. This view was shared by Cicero who thought that the study of Greek philosophy would improve aspiring politicians' moral character. He also believed that education should instil the Roman ideal of *civitas* – the Roman version of the Platonic ideal of an ordered society governed by reason. And just as Greek *paideia* was infused with the Homeric virtues of *arête,* so Cicero thought that the commitment to *civitas* would be strengthened by teaching the distinctively Roman virtue of *pietas* – a virtue that is expressed through a devotion to duty, patriotism and a respect for Roman ancestry and tradition.

Much like Greek *paideia*, the Roman education system was arranged in a number of stages. At the age of six, children were sent to private schools commonly known as *ludus litterarius* where a *litterator* – usually an educated Greek slave – would teach them the basics of reading, writing and arithmetic as well as the Greek language. Between nine and 12 years of age, boys from affluent families would leave their litterator to take up study with a *grammaticus*, who honed their writing and speaking skills, taught them Greek and Roman poetry and further improved their mastery of Greek. The next stage – the study of rhetoric – was largely confined to the children of the Roman elite who were destined for a legal or political career. As well as learning the art of public speaking, students would also be taught other subjects such as geography, music, literature, mythology and geometry. In the final stage of their education, they studied Greek philosophy at one or more of the four Hellenistic schools of philosophy that had been established during the fifth century BC to teach their own distinctive philosophies: Cynicism, Scepticism, Epicureanism and Stoicism.

While the Roman educational system adopted many Greek educational ideas and practices, there were some significant differences. Subjects that were fundamental to Greek *paideia*, like music and athletics, were dismissed by the Romans as irrelevant. Similarly, while the Greeks viewed a philosophical education as a defining characteristic of a civilised and educated person, the Romans saw philosophy as a distinctively Greek activity to be taught only insofar as it improved the orator's ability to develop a rationally compelling argument. But, regardless of these differences, the syncretism between their educational beliefs and practices further established the educational tradition initiated by Socrates, Plato and Aristotle. By the third century this tradition had spread to what became known as the 'Greco-Roman world': the many regions and countries under Roman rule that had more or less absorbed their ruler's culture.

One of the distinctive features of this culture was that it could accommodate the teaching of both religion and philosophy. Greek and Roman religions were both polytheistic, each tolerating many gods and religious myths. Also, while these myths often provided explanations about the mysteries of life and the origins of the world, they did not prescribe an authoritative set of religious edicts that all people had to follow and obey. On the contrary, both Greeks and Romans regarded questions about how individuals ought to live their lives as rational questions to be answered through the systematic study of philosophy. But in the 4th century BC, the Roman Empire officially embraced a monotheistic religion that prioritised religious faith over secular reason, and that was to hamper the progress of the Western educational tradition for the next thousand years.

References

Aristotle (1955) *The Nichomachean Ethics* (trans. J. A. K. Thomson) London: Penguin Classics.

Aristotle (1986) *the Politics.* London: Penguin Classics.

Homer. (2003a) *The Iliad.* London: Penguin Classics.

Homer. (2003b) *The Odyssey.* London. Penguin Classics.

Plato. (1974) *The Republic.* Harmondsworth: Penguin Classics.

Plato. (2012) *The Laws.* (trans. T. J. Saunders). London Penguin Classics.

4 Christianity

The Decline and Revival of the Western Educational Tradition

During the reign of the Roman Emperor Tiberius (14 BC–37 AD), an uneducated prophet from Galilee by the name of Jesus became the *Christos* – literally 'the anointed one' – for an obscure Jewish cult that would go on to shake the foundations of the most powerful empire the world had ever seen. What made these early Christians different from other religious sects was their insistence that there was only one god and that no other gods should be tolerated. At first, they were systematically persecuted but, following his conversion, Emperor Constantine the Great (272–337 AD) decriminalised Christianity and granted Christians the freedom to practice their religion. During the reign of Emperor Theodosius 1 (347–395 AD), Christianity was made the official state religion of the Roman Empire, non-Christian religious practices were prohibited by law, pagan temples were demolished and all other religious sects were declared heretical, an offence punishable by death. In 529 AD the ancient Greek philosophical schools that had been an important part of Roman education for over 500 years were put under the control of the Church which immediately denounced their teaching as anti-Christian and closed them down. Henceforth, the sacred texts of Christianity were to be the sole repository of knowledge and truth. Religious faith rather than human reason was now to guide people's lives. Philosophy was to be tolerated only insofar as it was made the handmaiden of theology.

The Christian obliteration of Greek philosophy was reinforced by the barbarian invasions that eventually destroyed the Roman Empire and its civilisation. In 410 BC the city of Rome was sacked by the Visigoth army, signalling the final disintegration of Roman authority and the fall of the Roman Empire. At the time, many Romans argued

DOI: 10.4324/9781003625735-4

that the main cause of their Empire's spectacular collapse was the official adoption of the Christian religion. But early in the fifth century this argument was vehemently rejected by the early Christian theologian and Neoplatonic philosopher, Augustine of Hippo (354–430 AD), in his masterpiece *On the City of God Against the Pagans*, often abbreviated to *The City of God* (2003).

Prior to his conversion, Augustine had been deeply influenced by Plato and Cicero, whose works he studied during his time as a professor of rhetoric in Milan. So, it is unsurprising that he used the Greek *polis* and the Roman *civitas* as examples of 'earthly cities' that stood in stark contrast to the heavenly 'City of God'. In essence, he argued that the fall of Rome was inevitable because, like all earthly cities, it was at the centre of a decadent, selfish and materialistic civilisation, immersed in the pleasures and preoccupations of a world that was devoid of meaning and purpose. Augustine contrasted this with the eternal City of God, which can only be inhabited after death by those who have forgone earthly pleasures and lived in accordance with God's wishes and commands. It was only by submitting to God's will in this earthly world that righteous people could enter this heavenly city and achieve eternal salvation.

The City of God quickly became the canonical text of early medieval Christian philosophy, expounding on theological questions, such as the existence of evil, the conflict between free will and divine omniscience and the doctrine of original sin. It was to provide the intellectual rationale for doctrinal beliefs that became ingrained in a mythical story about the origins of the world and the purpose of human existence that would be absorbed into the collective consciousness of Christians for centuries to come. This story can be summarised as follows.

God is our creator. He created us to know love, serve and obey him in this earthly world so that we can be eternally reconciled with him in his heavenly kingdom: the City of God. Because human nature is essentially weak and perverse, obeying God's will is not easy. As the inheritors of Adam's 'original sin', we are always vulnerable to the temptations of the flesh and liable to go astray. Our salivation depends on our being rescued from our corrupt human condition by the divine grace that is bestowed on us when our sinful appetites and desires are brought under the directing control of the commandments of an omniscient God.

This story became sufficiently entrenched in the hearts and minds of people from the diverse countries of Western Europe to allow the Christian Church to maintain its hegemonic dominance for the best part of a thousand years. It accomplished this remarkable feat by establishing a Christian elite invested with the power to impose universal allegiance to the Christian creed with totalitarian severity. Admission to this elite was confined to duly appointed church clergy: the divinely ordained bishops and priests who, as God's official representatives on earth, were responsible for spreading God's message, teaching prescribed Christian doctrines and performing various acts of worship. They gave sermons, conducted baptisms and marriage ceremonies, heard confessions and granted absolutions. As the intermediary between God and his people they exercised power over all aspects of peoples' lives from the cradle to the grave.

As Christianity became the established religion of the Western world, so the educational practices and institutions of the Roman Empire fell into decline. In medieval Christendom, all education was religious education and all teachers were either monks or priests. The Greek view that education is what enabled natural impulses and desires to be rationally cultivated and controlled was replaced by a view of education as a means of repressing impulses and desires so as to achieve unquestioning obedience to God's commands. As a result, developing the ability to reason that was so central to Greek and Roman education was rejected on the grounds that, unconstrained by Christian faith, human reason would be contaminated by a perverse will and lead to evil thoughts, sinful behaviour and heretical beliefs. By the fifth century, the educational tradition inherited from classical antiquity began to resemble an endangered species, hovering on the verge of extinction.

What prevented it from becoming totally obliterated was the emergence of the medieval monasteries. Originally monasteries were centres of asceticism entirely dedicated to the worship of God. But by the fourth century they had become important centres of scholarship, with monks copying and preserving sacred Christian texts and, significantly, the ancient philosophical works of classical antiquity. Throughout the early medieval period, monks were by far the best-educated members of society and usually the only people who could read and write. During the fifth century AD monasteries admitted young boys as *novicii* – trainee monks – who, prior to taking their religious vows, underwent an intense programme of study and prayer known as the *novitiate.* As the number of novicii increased, monasteries began to establish their own schools which, by the sixth century, also admitted children other than novices, usually boys of noble families who needed an education that would prepare them for high positions in church and state. By the eighth century, as well as teaching the *novitiate,* monastic schools started to teach a watered-down version of some of the academic subjects taught in ancient Greek *paideia.* These were divided into two groups: the *trivium* – grammar, rhetoric and dialectic; and the *quadrivium* – arithmetic, geometry, astronomy and music. In their Christianised form, these subjects were mere vestiges of what had been taught in Greek *paideia* and were simply used to facilitate the study of theology. For example, grammar was taught because it was useful for understanding ecclesiastical books; rhetoric as an aid to composing sermons; and dialectical reasoning as a method for refuting heresies.

Throughout the medieval period, monastic schools were complemented by cathedral schools that were originally established to train priests but also taught lay students, usually the children of noble families. At first the only teacher in the school was the bishop who, as well as passing on his religious knowledge, also taught trainee priests the rudiments of reading and writing. Over time, the bishop's responsibility for the work of the school was taken over by a *scholasticus* who was assisted by the group of priests initially responsible for performing the cathedral's liturgy. As in monastic schools, the curriculum was based on the seven subjects of the *trivium* and the *quadrivium*. But while the teaching of these subjects in monastic schools was superficial, cathedral schools made them the basis of an academically demanding programme of study intended for able and intelligent students. This programme was divided into two parts: *schola minor*, in which younger students were taught the *trivium*; and *schola major*, which provided older students with an advanced study of the *quadrivium.*

By the tenth century a more secular way of life had evolved across Europe, requiring a new breed of educated people not only to fill the administrative positions that were being created in the church and state but also to enter the expanding professions of law and medicine. Cathedral schools responded to this need by providing more advanced and diverse forms of education that would be appropriate to people other than potential priests. This resulted in them attracting large numbers of students from all over Europe, many of whom had no wish to pursue a career in the church but simply wanted a rigorous education that would satisfy their thirst for knowledge and passion for learning. With their rising popularity, cathedral schools began to surpass the monastic schools, both in number and importance. By the 11th century, they had become the major European centres of teaching, recruiting distinguished intellectuals and scholars to teach an ever-increasing number of able and enthusiastic students. As their numbers multiplied, these teachers and students gradually transformed themselves into academic guilds with their own customs and unwritten laws. Towards the end of the 11th century, they began to adopt an organisational structure known as a *univeritas*, which was derived from the Latin *universitas magistrorum et scholarium*, a community of teachers and scholars. So in Bologna (1088), Paris (1150), Oxford (1167), Modena (1175), Cambridge (1209) and Salamanca (1218) emerged a new educational institution: the university.

Because the early universities evolved from cathedral schools, it was inevitable that their curriculum would be based on the *trivium* and *quadrivium.* Students were initially admitted as `scholars' who attended lectures and responded to questions put by a teacher in a formal procedure, known as 'determination'. A student who had successfully 'determined' was given the status of a 'Bachelor of Arts' and could be granted a *licencia docendi* – a licence to teach. A bachelor who wished to qualify as a university teacher had to become a Master of Arts by spending anything from three to six years mastering the skills of their craft under the direction and supervision of a Master practitioner. The particular skills that an apprentice Master had to learn were those required to teach the Christian texts prescribed for the Bachelor of Arts degree. The first of these was the *lectio*, or lecture, a method for teaching the approved interpretation of these texts in a form which scholars could passively memorise and learn. But an apprentice also had to learn a new teaching method initially developed by a Peter Abelard (1079–1142 AD), a brilliant young philosopher and theologian who taught in Paris at the cathedral school of Notre Dame.

Abelard's teaching method provided students with a formalised method of debate designed to uncover and resolve apparent inconsistencies and contradictions in many of the established theological truths handed down by the Church Fathers. In his best-known philosophical work, *Sic et Non* (Yes and No) he listed 158 philosophical and theological questions and taught his students how to answer them by following the formal rules of *disputatio*, or disputation, a teaching method that had a lot in common with the dialectic method of reasoning that characterised classical Greek philosophy and, in particular, the Socratic method (Aberlard, 1978). Like the Socratic method, *disputatio* was a method for identifying and resolving contradictions in established beliefs through rational argument and an unrestrained search for truth. Like the Socratic method, it involved formulating questions and using dialectical reasoning to elicit arguments *pro* and *contra*. Just as Athenian politicians had accused Socrates of debasing the minds of the Athenian youth, so Christian theologians accused Abelard of encouraging students to question the truth of doctrinal orthodoxy. And just as Socrates was charged with corrupting the Athens youth, so Abelard was repeatedly charged with heresy.

Sic et Non was included in the Catholic Church's *Index of Forbidden Books*. But in the second half of the 13th century, a more benign version of *disputatio* was used by the Dominican scholar Thomas Aquinas (1225–1274) in his magisterial work *Summa Theologica* (1270), a book which is generally regarded as the greatest philosophical achievement of medieval Christendom (Aquinas, 1948). Drawing on the recently discovered works of Aristotle, the *Summa* proceeds through a series of formal disputations designed to assess the relative merits of religious faith and secular reason so as to achieve a synthesis between pagan philosophy and Christian theology. The *Summa* was written primarily as a text for theology students, so it is unsurprising that Aquinas concluded that, since faith and theology revealed truths that could not be discovered through rational inquiry, they took precedence over reason and philosophy.

Aquinas' brilliant synthesis of Aristotelian logic and Christian theology eventually came to define Christian philosophy. Following the publication of the *Summa* his reformulated version of *disputatio* was consolidated into a method of teaching and learning, known as 'scholasticism', that dominated university teaching from the 13th to the 16th century. The scholastic method was a highly formalised procedure that employed rigorous logic, a careful drawing of conceptual distinctions and the use of dialectic reasoning. But although it was supposed to provide scholars with the opportunity to think in more rational and critical ways, the scholastic method was so constrained by Christian orthodoxy that it only produced conclusions that were acceptable to the Catholic Church. Eventually, these constraints were seen as a barrier to any kind of rational inquiry or original thought. By the 14th century, many intellectuals began to suspect that scholasticism had degenerated into a sterile academic exercise, citing the famous scholastic question of 'how many angels can dance on the head of a pin?' as a prime example of the type of concerns theologians considered important but most people regarded as irrelevant and arcane. This eventually led many intellectuals to see scholasticism as impeding, rather than facilitating, rational inquiry and ask whether supplementing the study of Christian texts with a study of the pagan literature of classical antiquity might offer a better way to advance the pursuit of knowledge. So began the great revival of interest in classical art, literature and philosophy that characterised the period in European history known as the Renaissance.

The Renaissance began in 14th-century Florence, from where it quickly spread to the rest of Italy and then to the rest of Europe. The spirit of the Renaissance took many forms, but it is most clearly associated with the ideals and aspirations of humanism, an intellectual and cultural movement that was initiated by secular men of letters and became the defining feature of European cultural life for the best part of 300 years. The intellectual basis for Renaissance humanism derived from the Roman concept of *humanitas*, a political and educational ideal refined and developed by Marcus Tullius Cicero in the educational programme for orators set out in his *De Oratore* – translated as 'On the Ideal Orator' (2001). In essence, it gave expression to the radical idea that humanity, rather than Christianity, should be the main focus of intellectual, artistic, literary and other forms of cultural pursuit. Humanist thinkers thought that studying the classical literature of Greece and Rome, rather than the theological complexities of Christian doctrines, offered a more rational approach to questions about what it was to be human and what constituted a virtuous and morally worthwhile life. To this end, they aspired to develop a corpus of knowledge that would help humankind to break free from the strictures imposed by scholasticism, inspire free inquiry and create a new confidence in the possibilities of rational thought.

They pursued these aspirations by developing a form of education that echoed the ideals of Greek *paideia.* Like the Greeks, they believed that the purpose of education was to produce well-rounded, cultivated individuals who would seek to achieve excellence – *arête* – in their intellectual, artistic and physical activities. Those who lived up to this ideal were designated *Uomo Universale* – now translated as 'Renaissance Man', a term applied to gifted individuals of the age, the most renowned being Leonardo da Vinci (1452–1519 AD) whose achievements in art, science, music, invention and writing are legendary.

The first school dedicated to the formation of *Uomo Universale* was founded in 1443 by the humanist teacher Vittorino da Feltre (1378–1446), who had previously taught at the university of Padua. Feltre's school enrolled about 70 boys, mostly from noble families but some from poor families, who were chosen on the basis of their ability. Initially, students were taught to speak and write Latin in the ornate and complex style of Cicero – a style that was very different from the more functional Latin of the medieval university. They were also given a firm grounding in *ars dictaminis* – the art of prose composition – as well as the art of writing letters. After completing these preliminary requirements, students were taught *Studia Humanitatis* – the study of humanity – which included classical literature, history, poetry, rhetoric, moral philosophy, arithmetic, Greek and some modern foreign languages. Many of the classical texts used to teach these subjects were written by Greeks but some were by Roman authors and written in Latin. For this reason, humanist schools were frequently called 'Latin schools', though in England they were more commonly known as 'grammar schools'. Many present-day English public schools – for example, Eton, Harrow, Rugby and Winchester – were initially humanist grammar schools set up to educate gifted and talented boys from relatively poor backgrounds. By the beginning of the 16th century, Latin and grammar schools were providing a humanist education for virtually the entire European elite, producing well-educated, cultivated and compassionate individuals who could speak, argue and write with eloquence and erudition and had the moral and intellectual qualities that would inspire them to participate in the civic life of their society.

Although most humanist teachers and scholars were devout Christians, many were highly critical of the Catholic Church's dour fixation on human depravity as well as the corruption infecting all aspects of ecclesiastical life. Towards the end of the 15th century, some of them combined their humanist and Christian beliefs to create what was to become the dominant philosophy of northern Europe, Christian Humanism: a philosophy based on the belief that human dignity and personal self-fulfilment offered a more optimistic guide to the Christian way of life. One of the earliest Christian humanists was John Colet (1467–1519), an English Catholic scholar, theologian and priest, who founded St Paul's School. But its most influential exponent was the Dutch Catholic priest Erasmus of Rotterdam (1469–1536) who, as well as being one of the greatest Renaissance philosophers, was also amongst the Catholic Church's fiercest internal critics. He condemned the widespread corruption amongst bishops and priests, ridiculed scholasticism and criticised many Catholic doctrines, not least the Augustinian doctrine of human depravity and original sin. But, despite his withering criticisms, Erasmus remained a member of the Catholic Church, committed to reforming it from within by advancing a Christian humanist educational philosophy that would combine the spirit of early Christianity with humanism's optimistic view of human nature.

Erasmus outlined his educational philosophy in three treatises: *De Ratione Studii* (On the Method of Study, 1978b); *Institutio Principis Christiani* (*The Education of a Christian Prince*) (1997); and *De Pueris Instituendis* (*On the Education of Children*, (2004)). In these, he reformulated ideas drawn from classical philosophy to support a form of Christian education that emphasised cooperative, rather than coercive, teaching methods, the importance of learning Greek and Latin and the need to study classical texts as well as the Bible. He also drew on the works of Quintilian and Cicero to suggest that memorisation and imitation – the prominent methods of instruction at the time – should be replaced by methods that recognised the importance of rational argument in the interpretation of both classical and religious texts. In contrast to scholasticism, he prioritised ethics over logic and the formation of moral character over the acquisition of theological knowledge. To reinforce his educational philosophy, he published numerous textbooks emphasising the importance of erudition, eloquence and cultural edification, most notably his hugely popular *On Copia* (1978a), which taught students how to argue, write and revise texts; and 'On the Writing of Letters' (1985), which taught them how best to write letters and use eloquent expressions.

Throughout the 16th century the efforts to implement Erasmus' educational ideas were beset by the obvious contradictions arising from Christian Humanism's attempt to integrate religious and secular beliefs. The task of resolving these contradictions was taken up by the Society of Jesus, a religious order founded in 1543 by Ignatius of Loyola (1491–1556), a military nobleman from the Basque region of Spain. The Society was originally established to preserve and propagate the Catholic faith by sending missionaries to convert heathens in a diverse range of regions across the world. Later, it would play a major role in the Counter-Reformation, with Jesuits acting as self-proclaimed 'soldiers of God' in the Catholic Church's battle against Protestantism. But the main way it fulfilled its evangelical mission was by establishing Catholic schools, first in Europe and then throughout the rest of the world. In 1548, ten members of the Society opened the first Jesuit school in Messina in Sicily. By 1556 this number had risen to over a 100 and by 1610 to over 300. In 1654 the Society opened the so-called Roman College, which soon developed into the Pontifical Gregorian University. By 1773, Jesuits were running over 800 schools, colleges and universities across the world. It was the largest educational organisation the world had ever seen.

The Jesuits did not think that their unqualified loyalty to the Catholic Church was incompatible with humanist ideals. Nor did they believe that humanist education and medieval scholasticism were irreconcilable. Instead, they saw them as complementary, recognising how the intellectual rigour of the scholastic method enhanced the skills of detached argument and logical analysis while, at the same time, acknowledging how a humanist education infused students with the ideal of service to the common good. In 1559 they incorporated their own particular version of Christian Humanism into the *Ratio atque Institutio Studiorum Societatis Iesu* ('The Official Plan for Jesuit Education'), that merged a commitment to *Christiana* – the art of Christian living –with a commitment to the classical Roman concept of *pietas* – a devotion to civic duty and the common good (Society of Jesus, 2005). But the *Ratio's* practical purpose was to stipulate how Jesuit educational institutions should operate by giving a detailed job description for everybody who worked in a Jesuit school. For teachers, it set out the prescribed texts they were to teach, the order in which they were to be taught and the methods used to teach them. It also stipulated that Jesuit schools should be organised into lower schools, which provided a seven-year term of instruction, and higher schools or seminaries, with a six-year term of instruction. The former was to offer a modified version of *Studia Humanitatis* which would serve as preparation for entry to the higher school that would follow a rigorous academic curriculum based on the scholastic education offered by medieval universities. The *Ratio Studiorum* was the first serious attempt to standardise what schools should teach, who should teach it and how it should be taught. It was adopted by Jesuit schools across the world and served as a unifying force for Jesuit education for almost 200 years.

Early in the Renaissance period, the Italian poet and scholar Francesco Petrarch (1304–1374) characterised the 900 years following the fall of the Roman Empire as the 'Dark Ages', a period of intellectual stagnation and cultural decline in which the 'darkness' induced by ignorance and religious superstition prevented Greek and Roman philosophy from seeing the light of day. It is therefore unsurprising to find that the history of education during this period is a history of how, after facing something approaching total obliteration, the Western education tradition somehow managed to survive. This process of resuscitation began when monastic schools began to teach the secular subjects of the *trivium* and *quadrivium.* It was further aided and assisted during the 12th and 13th centuries when the scholastic method of *disputatio* was tentatively and cautiously used to bring the power of human reason to bear on Christian beliefs. And it was dramatically revived during the 15th and 16th centuries when Renaissance humanists drew on the rediscovered literature of classical antiquity to develop a form of education based on *Studia Humanitatis* that would inspire a renewed confidence in the humanising potential of rational thought.

So, although the history of this period is a story of how the Western educational tradition was almost extinguished, it is also a story of how its fundamental assumption about the intrinsic relationship between education and the development of reason was kept alive. But during the 17th and 18th centuries, the power and authority of Christian theology finally began to disintegrate under the impact of a set of scientific, philosophical and political ideas that restored and reinvigorated the Western educational tradition and radically transformed our understanding of how its aims and aspirations should be pursued. To distinguish it from the preceding age of religious faith, this period is sometimes called 'the Age of Reason'. But, because it was seen as offering the 'light' that would finally bring the Dark Ages to an end, it is more commonly known as 'the Age of Enlightenment'.

References

Abelard, P. (1978) *Sic et Non.* Chicago: Chicago University Press.
Aquinas, T. (1948) *Summa Theologica.* Indiana: Ave Maria Press.
Augustine of Hippo. (2003) *City of God.* London: Penguin Classics.
Cicero, M. T. (2001) *On the Ideal Orator*. Oxford: Oxford University Press.

Erasmus, D. (1978a) *On Copia.* (Collected Works of Erasmus, Vol. 24. Ed. C. R. Thompson.) Toronto, ON: University of Toronto Press.

Erasmus, D. (1978b) 'On the Method of Study' in *Collected Works of Erasm*us, Vol. 23. ed. C. R. Thompson. Toronto: University of Toronto Press.

Erasmus, D. (1985). 'On the Writing of Letters' in *Collected Works of Erasmus.* Vol. 24. ed. J. K. Sowards. Toronto University Press Toronto.

Erasmus, D. (1997). *The Education of a Christian Prince.* Cambridge: Cambridge University Press.

Erasmus, D. (2004) *On the Education of Children.* Madrid: Hard Press.

Society of Jesus. (2005) *The Ratio Studiorum: the Official Plan for Jesuit Education.* St. Louis: Institute of Jesuit Sources (Internet Archive).

5 The Enlightenment and the Emergence of Progressive Education

As he lay on his deathbed, the Polish astronomer and mathematician Nicolaus Copernicus (1473–1543) read the proofs of his great work *De revolutionibus orbium coelestium libri VI* ('Six Books Concerning the Revolutions of the Heavenly Orbs') in which he had advanced the then heretical view that the sun, rather than the earth, was at the centre of the solar system (Copernicus, 1995). This not only contradicted the universally held belief that the sun revolved around the earth; it also conflicted with the teachings of the Catholic Church which regarded it as contrary to Scripture and incompatible with the science of theology. Over 70 years later, the refusal of the Italian astronomer Galileo Galilei (1564–1642) to reject Copernicus' theory led to his being officially admonished by the Church. When in his *Dialogue Concerning the Two Chief World Systems* (Galileo, 1962) he again endorsed Copernicus' theory, Galileo was summonsed to appear before the Inquisition, where he was convicted of heresy, forced to recant and sentenced to spend the rest of his life under house arrest. Three years later his book joined Copernicus's book on the *Index Librorum Prohibitorum* – the Catholic Church's official list of banned books – where it remained for the next 200 years.

Then, as now, banning books made people want to read them even more, and Copernicus' and Galileo's books marked the starting point of a revolution that transformed the subsequent history of humankind. This revolution – the Scientific Revolution – gave birth to a new method of scientific inquiry that would eventually replace the way of investigating the natural world known as 'natural philosophy', a subject studied in the Arts faculties of medieval universities. In their inquiries, natural philosophers employed the scholastic method of

DOI: 10.4324/9781003625735-5

disputatio either to dispute theological questions arising from the account of the natural world provided in Aristotle's *Physics* or to resolve contradictions between the Christian and the Aristotelian conception of nature. The main achievement of the Scientific Revolution was to transform science from a branch of speculative philosophy into a method for discovering knowledge that depended on nothing other than neutral observation and independent rational thought.

The chief architect of this method was the English philosopher and statesman Francis Bacon (1561–1626) who, like many other British intellectuals, thought that natural philosophy was a practically useless discipline that simply fostered argument for its own sake. He also castigated natural philosophers whose reliance on sophisticated logical argument never discovered anything new and served only to retard the growth of scientific knowledge. In 1620, he published *Novum Organum* – 'The New Organon' – in which he argued that the only way to overcome these deficiencies was to develop a way of answering scientific questions that, if correctly applied, would produce valid knowledge (Bacon, 1978). To this end, he formulated a method of inquiry that used observation, experimentation and inductive reasoning to discover facts that could be used to uncover the laws of nature. At first natural philosophers greeted Bacon's suggestion that they should collect facts with astonishment. But, despite this initial reaction, Bacon's scientific method provided the catalyst for the creation, in 1662, of the Royal Society of London for the Promotion of Natural Knowledge. In 1687 the Society's most illustrious member – Sir Isaac Newton – published *Philosophiae Naturalis Principia Mathematica* ('Mathematical Principles of Natural Philosophy') that finally put the theories of Copernicus and Galileo beyond any rational doubt (Newton, 2020). It also supplied the final push in the battle to create a method that would replace scholastic argument with observation and experimentation and so enable scientific inquiries to be conducted in exclusively rational and empirical terms.

As well as replacing natural philosophy, Bacon's method raised the question of whether philosophy in general needed to adopt a distinctive method of reasoning that would validate the truth of its claims to knowledge. It is therefore no accident that, at about the same time as Bacon was advocating a strictly rational scientific method, the French philosopher Rene Descartes (1596–1650) published *Discourse on Method*, which sets out a philosophical method that was to transform philosophy from the 'handmaiden of theology' into a mode of inquiry that was independent of Christian doctrines and beliefs (Descartes, 1968) This method simply required philosophers to refuse to accept the truth of any claim to knowledge unless it can be shown to be beyond all possible doubt. After first systematically doubting everything he could conceivably doubt, Descartes realised that the only thing he could not doubt – and, hence, the only thing he could know with any certainty – is that he is doubting! From this he argued that since 'doubting' is a specific kind of thinking, and since he cannot think without acknowledging his own existence, the only certain knowledge he has is that he exists, an inference cogently expressed in one of the most famous sentences in the entire history of philosophy, *Cogito ergo sum* – 'I think, therefore I am.'

Descartes' method of systematic doubt was to revolutionise western philosophy and exert immense influence over the development of modern philosophical thought. But, together with the Scientific Revolution, its immediate effect was to prepare the ground for a period in the intellectual history of Europe that is usually referred to as 'the Enlightenment'. There is little consensus about when the Enlightenment began but many historians trace its origins to the middle of the 18th century when a loosely organised group of French intellectuals known as *Les Philosophes* began to advance the idea that the power of human reason could emancipate individuals from ignorance, dogma and superstition and so enable them to transform themselves and the world in which they live. This celebration of the beneficial effects of human reason was to become central to all aspects of Enlightenment thought. It underwrote its advocacy of individual freedom, equality, democracy and religious tolerance as well as its claim that rational knowledge acquired through the application of the scientific method would enhance the happiness and well-being of humankind.

Throughout the second half of the 18th century these ideas were discussed in Parisian literary salons and coffeehouses and eventually disseminated across Europe through the published writings of *Les Philosophes*, most notably Voltaire (1694–1778), Montesquieu (1689–1755) and Condorcet (1743–1794). But the most famous interpretation of the meaning of 'Enlightenment' was provided by the German philosopher Immanuel Kant (1724–1804). In his essay '*Answering the Question: What Is Enlightenment?*' he recognised that the basic metaphor of the Enlightenment – that of light – was intended to convey the message that humanity has now reached a stage in its evolution that made it possible for human reason to illuminate the darkness of ignorance and superstition imposed by the religious and political institutions of the old despotic order (Kant, 2009). He therefore characterised the Enlightenment as the historical period during which humankind was finally in a position to abandon its 'self-incurred immaturity', a condition that was entirely due to people's reluctance to use their own reason rather than following the spoon-fed dogmas of church and state. For Kant, the motto of the Enlightenment – *Sapere aude!* ('Dare to be wise!') – was intended to convey the message that the time has come for people to throw off the yoke of ignorance and have the courage to think and act as rationally autonomous individuals capable of thinking, acting and choosing for themselves. Once freed from the irrational constraints of prejudice, dogma and tradition, humanity would have finally completed its long period of immaturity. Human reason would then become an objective historical force, guiding the conduct of individuals and making the world a better place.

Kant recognised that human reason does not operate naturally or instinctively and can only be realised in a certain kind of society and through a certain kind of education. This provided Enlightenment philosophers with two closely related tasks. The first was to articulate a philosophical rationale for a society whose laws are formulated by its individual members collectively exercising their own power of rational thought. The second was to articulate a form of education that would encourage individuals to think for themselves and thereby empower them to participate in creating the kind of society that gave them the freedom to act on the basis of their own autonomous reason. Both these tasks were eloquently and passionately undertaken by one of the greatest of all Enlightenment philosophers: Jean-Jacques Rousseau (1712–1778).

The simple, overriding idea at the centre of all Rousseau's thinking was that human beings are naturally good, and the Christian doctrine of original sin is false. For Rousseau, human depravity was not an innate condition but simply a reflection of the extent to which natural human goodness had been corrupted by the religious and political institutions of civilised society. In his essay *Discourse on Inequality* (1758) he explained how this occurred by constructing a history of the social evolution of humanity that begins with the emergence of *Homo sapiens* and ends with the arrival of civilisation (Rousseau, 1984). He argued that throughout this period humans, like all other animals, lived 'according to nature', instinctively driven by basic survival needs for food, warmth, shelter and self-preservation. However, Rousseau believed that, unlike most other members of the animal world, humans had a natural disposition of compassion or empathy: a disposition to relieve the suffering of fellow humans as well as other animals. As they evolved and became more conscious of themselves as social beings, this became manifest in an altruistic desire to take care of other members of their social group which, in turn, led them to have an allegiance to their society's common good. But with the emergence of civilisation, humanity became egoistic, selfish and self-interested and, as a result, the freedom to pursue the common good was more or less suppressed. The task Rousseau set for himself was to find a viable way for humanity to regain the simplicity of original human nature and so reinstate the natural desire for freedom. Four years after the publication of the *Discourse on Inequality* he offered two routes to achieving this end, one political the other educational.

The political route is set out in Rousseau's most famous work, *The Social Contract* (1762), a book that begins with a dramatic announcement: 'Man is born free and everywhere is in chains' (Rousseau, 1968). Since the 'chains' constraining human freedom are those imposed by the oppressive religious and political institutions characterising modern civilisation, the only feasible way of restoring natural freedom is for members of civil society to enter a 'social contract' by which they only agree to accept laws restricting their natural freedom on condition that they themselves participate in their formulation and collectively agree to impose them on themselves. In such a society, the legitimacy of political authority would stem from the fact that it serves the common good of all society's members as encapsulated in what Rousseau calls the 'General Will'. It is only in a society in which political authority rests on the consent of all its citizens that natural freedom can be preserved.

Rousseau recognised that in society as it existed at the time, people would be reluctant to subordinate their private interests to the common good. He therefore felt it necessary to confront fundamental questions about how to educate future generations to create and maintain a society that promotes, rather than supresses, natural freedom. In 1762, he set out his answer to this question in *Émile, ou De l'éducation* ('Émile, or On Education' (1974), a book Rousseau himself considered to be "the best and most important of all his writings" (Rousseau, 1953, p.529–30).

Émile opens with a powerful assertion: 'Everything is good as it leaves the hands of the Author of things; everything degenerates in the hands of man.' Rousseau responds to this predicament by describing how a young child, Émile, should be educated to become a rational and moral member of a civilised society while remaining true to his original nature. To this end, Émile is immediately removed from the corrupting influence of society to a world inhabited only by himself and his private tutor. During Émile's infancy the tutor's main task is to make him 'nature's pupil' – by ensuring that all his learning is guided by his own emotions and natural inclinations. The tutor does not tell Émile what to do or think but simply acts as a guide helping him to learn from his self-chosen explorations and first-hand experiences. The second stage of his education starts at the end of infancy and continues to the age of 12. During this, his tutor refrains from any direct instruction but instead continues to encourage Émile to learn through experience.

It is only during the third stage of his education that Émile begins to develop his innate ability to reason. Like other Enlightenment philosophers, Rousseau accepted that developing the capacity to reason was a fundamental educational aim. As he put it, 'The noblest work in education is to make a reasoning man … if children understood how to reason they would not need to be educated' (1974, p.53). He also regarded the view of children as miniature adults who could be taught how to reason through a process of instruction as tantamount to 'talking to them … in a language they do not understand' (1974, p.53). 'Childhood', he wrote, 'has its own way of seeing, thinking and feeling … I should no more expect judgement in a ten year old child than I should expect him to be five feet high … ' (1974, p.54) 'Childhood', he famously asserted, 'is the sleep of reason' (1974, p.55).

Because Émile's reason remains dormant throughout childhood, his tutor does not try to rouse his 'sleeping' reason until he has reached adolescence. Rousseau of course rejected any suggestion that human reason can be developed through a process of instruction, rote learning or studying books. Instead, the general rule governing this stage in Émile's education is 'learning by doing' and is designed to encourage him to use his ability to reason to solve practical problems in natural settings. The final stage of Émile's education begins when he is 16 and involves a historical study of other societies and cultures and extensive instruction in political philosophy. At the end of this stage, Émile has reached 'the age of reason', which culminates in him recognising how his education has prepared him to be a rational member of a society based on the Social Contract and guided by the General Will.

The publication of *Émile* was greeted with widespread outrage and Rousseau was accused of inciting moral turpitude by prioritising primitive passions over godly love. In Paris, *Émile* was banned and copies of the book publicly burned. Nevertheless, throughout the 19th century, Rousseau's radical ideas – about, for example, human goodness, the nature of childhood, the role of the teacher and 'learning from experience' – inspired a number of notable educationalists. One of the earliest of these was the Swiss pedagogue Heinrich Pestalozzi (1746–1827) who wrote many works explaining his own educational philosophy. His main educational treatise, *My Inquiries into the Course of Nature in the Development of Mankind*, was heavily influenced by Rousseau's belief that education should be geared to the natural unfolding of the child's development (Pestalozzi, 1946). In 1805 he set up a boarding school at Yverdon in Switzerland with a curriculum modelled on Rousseau's plan for Émile. Although Pestalozzi emphasised group learning he made allowances for individual differences, grouping children according to their aptitudes and ability rather than age.

The Yverdon Institute attracted many foreign visitors, the most famous being the German educator Friedrich Froebel (1782–1852). In 1826 he published his most important treatise, *Menschenerziehung* ('The Education of Man'), a philosophical rationale for the educational methods he put into practice at the infant school he opened in Blankenburg, Prussia, called the 'garden of children', or kindergarten (Froebel, 2005). The most radical feature of the kindergarten was that it replaced direct instruction and rote learning with teaching methods that encouraged children to learn through play. To this end, Froebel devised circles, spheres and other toys as well as a range of learning activities that were based on songs and music. He also started a publishing firm to produce other educational materials with lengthy explanations of how they were to be used. These publications proved to be immensely popular and were translated into several foreign languages. Soon Froebel's ideas were attracting the attention of educators in England, France, Netherlands and the United States, where the kindergarten movement was to achieve its greatest success.

Rousseau's declaration of the innate goodness of human nature, his insights into the distinctive nature of childhood and his understanding of how the child's capacity to reason only emerged slowly in the course of their natural development, inspired Pestalozzi, Froebel and other educators to formulate a 'progressive' view of education that stressed the educational importance of children's needs and interests and gave notions such as 'learning from experience' and 'the teacher as a guide' a central place. By the end of the 19th century, as progressive education evolved into a full-blown pedagogical movement, many of the unquestioned assumptions and beliefs previously incorporated in the Western educational tradition became the subject of intense argument about how its aims and ideals should be pursued. In the main, this argument focussed on the very different answers provided by Plato and Rousseau to fundamental questions about what and how to teach and who should be educated. The classical Platonic view prioritised the teaching of academic knowledge; progressive educators argued that what should be taught should be determined by reference to children's own needs and interests. Classical education cast the teacher in the role of an instructor transmitting a predetermined body of academic knowledge; progressive education portrayed the teacher as a guide, helping children to enhance the quality of their learning experiences. Progressive educators regarded the Platonic assumption that only an academic elite is capable of being educated as a prime example of the kind of elitism that the Enlightenment sought to destroy.

Because these conflicts and disagreements occurred *within* the Western educational tradition, they stimulated the kind of arguments and debates that allowed that tradition to be critically revised and progressively evolve. But throughout the 19th century, the impact of progressive educational ideas was frustrated and impaired by the emergence of a system of education that was neither classical nor progressive, owed nothing to the Western educational tradition and was oblivious to the ideal of human reason championed by the Enlightenment. The name of this new educational phenomenon is 'schooling'.

References

Bacon, F. (1978) *The New Organon.* Cambridge: Cambridge University Press.

Copernicus, N. (1995) *On the Revolutions of Heavenly Spheres.* New York: Prometheus Books.

Descartes, R. (1968) *Discourse on Method and Meditations on First Philosophy* (trans. F. E. Sutcliffe) London: Penguin.

Froebel, F. (2005) *The Education of Man New York:* Dover Publications.

Galileo, G. (1962) *Dialogue Concerning the Two Chief World Systems.* Oakland: University of California Press.

Kant, I. (2009) *An Answer to the Question: 'What Is Enlightenment?'* London: Penguin Classics.

Newton, I. (2020) *The Mathematical Principles of Natural Philosophy.* London: Flame Tree.

Pestalozzi, J. H. (1946) 'My Inquiries into the Course of Nature in the Development of Mankind'. In *Complete Works and Letters; Critical Education*, ed. Emanuel Dejung. Zurich: Orell Fussli Verlag.

Rousseau, J-J. (1953) *The Confessions*. Trans. J.M. Cohen. New York: Penguin. Rousseau, J-J. (1968) *The Social Contract.* Harmondsworth: Penguin Classics.

Rousseau, J-J. (1974) *Émile, On Education.* London: Dent.

Rousseau, J-J. (1984) *Discourse on Inequality.* London: Penguin Classics.

6 Education and State Schooling

Before the 18th century, nearly all European countries were part of multi-ethnic kingdoms with no shared language or common culture. But the combined effect of various political developments led to their gradual reconfiguration into nation states: geographically bound self-governing countries inhabited by law-abiding citizens who shared the same language, history, culture and traditions. What these newly formed nations quickly realised was that the most effective way to establish and sustain their national identity was to establish compulsory education systems charged with forming patriotic citizens who collectively identified themselves as belonging to a particular state. These were first introduced in Prussia and France and soon appeared in Greece, Denmark, Iceland Sweden, Norway, Switzerland, Spain and Italy.

However, these state schooling systems varied dramatically. This was largely due to the fact that the political upheavals caused by the French Revolution had provided fertile ground for the emergence of both revolutionary and counter-revolutionary social movements, each advocating a distinctive doctrine about the goals that nation states should adopt and the kind of government best suited to their achievement. These doctrines quickly morphed into a range of political ideologies – such as nationalism, liberalism, democracy, socialism and communism – each incorporating a particular understanding of how compulsory schooling could be used to advance the ideological interests of the state. And, as different systems of state schooling were enlisted in the service of rival political ideologies, a proliferation of incompatible *political* conceptions of education became a dominant feature of the 19th-century educational landscape.

DOI. 10.4324/9781003625735-6

Prior to the emergence of nation states, education throughout western Europe was more or less the same. But as different states embraced different political ideologies, their schooling systems developed along different paths and at a different pace. The obvious implication of this is that any attempt to portray the subsequent history of Western education as more than an amalgam of these disparate developments is virtually impossible. It is for this reason that the remainder of this book will concentrate on the development of education in England, where state schooling was introduced in the second half of the 19th century to serve a political ideology that had taken root during the 18th century: classical liberalism.

Classical liberalism's central beliefs were most clearly articulated in Adam Smith's *The Wealth of Nations,* published in 1776, and Jeremy Bentham's *An Introduction to the Principles of Morals and Legislation*, published in 1780 (Bentham, 2009; Smith, 2012). The most fundamental of these was the belief in 'liberal individualism': the belief that the political and economic freedom of individuals was paramount and should be protected from state interference by limiting government power to national defence, the protection of private property and the maintenance of law and order. Accompanying this belief in the 'minimal state' was a fervent advocacy of laissez-faire economic doctrines and a deep-seated aversion to state-provided welfare services of any kind. Initially, this meant that, from a classical liberal perspective, any state involvement in education would be construed as an affront to individual liberty and undermine the moral responsibility of parents for their children's education. However, this belief began to crumble under the pressure to come to terms with the profound political and economic changes set in motion by the Industrial Revolution that began in England sometime around the 1750s. By the end of the 18th century, this had led to the hierarchical social system that had previously secured the power and privileges of a landed aristocracy being replaced by a system based on the notion of 'class', with the dominant distinctions being between the aristocratic upper class, the middle class and the lower working class.

By the beginning of the 19th century, the population explosion caused by industrialisation had created vast urban working-class centres, such as Manchester and Birmingham, where crime and violence were endemic and social unrest could easily flourish. At the same time, the spread among the working classes of the subversive ideas that had fuelled the French Revolution was seen as a potential source of civil disobedience and mob rule. The proposed solution to both of these threats was to provide working-class children with an elementary education that would teach them to respect their betters, reconcile them to their station in life and so make them less likely to engage in political protest or social unrest.

From the outset, then, the official rationale for educating working-class children was social control: to teach them the kind of knowledge, values and attitudes necessary to ensure that they passively accepted their allotted social and economic roles. This was to be achieved by teaching them a modicum of useful knowledge, a respect for authority and a belief in the Christian religion. At first, offering even this minimal level of education to working class children was opposed, particularly by members of the aristocracy, on the grounds that it was unnecessary and undesirable. It was unnecessary because they did not need to be educated in order to perform their allocated role in the social order. It was undesirable because it had the potential to be socially disruptive by teaching the poor to despise their lot in life and no longer defer to their social superiors. But although the view that educating working-class children was an important way of combating social unrest eventually prevailed, the climate of opinion created by classical liberalism's fierce opposition to state involvement in education meant that any educational expansion would have to be accomplished through the efforts of voluntary organisations.

The organisations that emerged to meet this requirement were The Anglican National Society for Promoting the Education of the Poor in the Principles of the Established Church, which was founded in 1811, and the non-denominational British and Foreign Society, founded in 1815. The National schools, founded by Andrew Bell, emphasised deference, the importance of social hierarchy and the acceptance of one's allocated station in life. The nonconformist British schools, founded by Joseph Lancaster, stressed humility, discipline, obedience and self-improvement. Although Bell and Lancaster were antagonistic towards each other, they pioneered a system of elementary schooling which provided a form of mass education that was highly consistent with the political and economic climate of the time. This system – the monitorial system – was to dominate mass schooling for the remainder of the 19th century.

The essence of the monitorial system was that it was economical and mechanical. It was economical because a school would only need to employ a single teacher who would instruct older pupils – or 'monitors' – who would then instruct a small group of about 10 younger children, with the teacher acting as a supervisor, examiner and disciplinarian. A school with one teacher would often have around 500 pupils who would be accommodated in a large single room filled with approximately 25 rows of desks each accommodating about 20 children. Learning was wholly mechanical, relying entirely on the memorisation of factual information and learning by rote. Children had no opportunity to ask questions or display any individual initiative. They were simply drilled in the rudiments of reading, writing, arithmetic and the Christian religion by monitors who had themselves been drilled by a teacher. In the prevailing classical liberal culture, the monitorial system was widely praised as an economical and efficient piece of social machinery that resonated with the industrial spirit of the time. Indeed, it simply transferred all the characteristics of a factory into an educational setting: a division of labour; an assembly line with children were passed on from one monitor to another; an impersonal system of inspection and testing; and strict attention given to cost-effectiveness and the efficient use of resources.

Although, by the middle of the 1830s, monitorial schools were catering for well over a million children, they could not keep pace with the growing demand. In 1833 the government, somewhat reluctantly, agreed to grant an annual sum of £20,000 to the National and British Societies towards the cost of new elementary school buildings on condition that half the cost was met from voluntary contributions. By 1853 this figure had increased to £250,000 per annum and, by 1859, it had reached over £750,000. Because of the government's general reluctance to spend taxpayers' money on education, this rapid increase in expenditure made it necessary to find a way to further increase the number of elementary schools without increasing spending. To this end, it set up a Royal Commission 'to inquire into the Present State of Popular Education in England and to consider what measures are required for the Extension of Sound and Cheap Elementary Instruction'. In its Report of 1861, the Newcastle Report, as it came to be known, found that the 'present state' of elementary education was beset by irregular attendance and low levels of learning. Its 'sound and cheap' solution was to replace the existing system of annual educational grants with a system of payments that depended on the attendance record of pupils and their performance in examinations.

This system of 'payment by results' was introduced in 1863 in the form of the 'Revised Code' that made the size of the government grants paid to individual schools conditional on their pupils' performance in reading, writing and arithmetic tests. To demonstrate that pupils had been effectively taught, the Revised Code laid down a syllabus of work graded according to six age-related 'standards'. A pupil who achieved the required standard in a test conducted by a government inspector would earn the school eight shillings. Failure would reduce the grant by 2 shillings and 6 pence. An 'attendance grant' of 4 shillings was also paid for each child attending school for a minimum of 200 half-day sessions per year. In recommending the Revised Code to the House of Commons, Robert Lowe, who was Vice-President of the Committee of the Council on Education, famously quipped 'If it is not cheap it shall be efficient; if it is not efficient it shall be cheap' (Maclure, 1986, p.79).

Although payment by results lasted, with modifications, for nearly 40 years, it did little to increase the provision of elementary schooling. By the end of the 1860s, as the demand for more elementary schools continued to increase, arguments for a coordinated state-provided system of elementary schooling system finally began to be taken seriously. In 1870 the government introduced the Elementary Education Act which, for the first time, acknowledged the state's responsibility for the provision of basic elementary education. The Act set up locally-elected School Boards with the power to fill the gaps in the existing voluntary system by levying rates to fund new elementary schools. By 1880 attendance at elementary schools was made more or less compulsory. In 1896, there were over 2 million children in the new 'Board' schools and a similar number in voluntary schools. As the 19th century drew to a close, the foundations for a state system of mass schooling specifically designed to offer a minimal standard of instruction for a specific social class had been firmly put in place.

Certainly, the system of 'payment by results' produced the desired reductions in government expenditure. It was also highly effective in providing working-class children with the minimum rudiments in reading, writing and arithmetic as cheaply as possible. But its educational consequences were disastrous. By tying government funding to test results in a limited range of subjects, it made learning rigid and narrow. By forcing teachers to concentrate on the grant-awarding potential of their pupils, it ensured that any ideas about introducing progressive teaching methods were quickly supressed. And, by fostering rote learning and the memorisation of facts, it rendered examination results virtually meaningless in educational terms.

Throughout the period when a state-provided system of elementary education was being established, secondary schools remained free from any kind of state interference or control. In keeping with classical liberalism's emphasis on individual freedom, it was simply taken for granted that parents had a right to pass on their economic and social privileges by sending their children to fee-paying private schools. Many of these were the public grammar schools founded during the Renaissance to provide a humanist education for local children. But once it was realised that these schools played a major role in maintaining existing patterns of privilege, they were removed from local control and became fee-paying residential schools exclusively reserved for the children of the aristocratic elite.

The statutes under which most endowed grammar schools had initially been established obliged them to focus exclusively on teaching classical subjects. However, at the beginning of the 19th century, as they began to accept children of the newly enriched industrial middle classes, this curriculum was seen as too narrow to cater for the needs of a growing industrial society. In 1840, these restrictions were removed by the Grammar Schools Act, which made it lawful for grammar schools to modernise their curriculum to include subjects that would appeal to the new middle classes, such as English literature, mathematics, science and modern foreign languages.

During the second half of the 19th century, it became apparent that the number of endowed grammar schools was insufficient to meet the demands of a rapidly expanding middle class. In its survey of secondary school provision published in 1868, the Taunton Commission not only confirmed that there were not enough grammar schools but also found large variations in what they provided. It therefore proposed that they should be classified on the basis of three grades. This proposal was adopted by the Bryce Commission, set up in 1894 to consider the organisation of a national system of secondary education. It proposed three types of secondary schools: 'first grade' schools, which included the famous public schools, offering a classical education to the children of the aristocracy; 'second grade' schools, which included some endowed grammar schools, preparing middle-class children for occupations in commerce or trade; and 'third grade' schools, which included both endowed schools and private schools, preparing lower middle-class children for specialised craft occupations.

Acting on the Bryce Commission's recommendations, the Education Act of 1902 formally stratified secondary education into public schools, grammar schools and third grade schools. It also established a comprehensive system of Local Educational Authorities with the legal authority to set up new secondary schools, supervise existing grammar schools and provide free places for working-class children. It led to the creation of over 1,000 new 'municipal' or 'county' secondary schools, including 349 for girls. In 1904 the government brought in the 'Regulations for Secondary Schools', which prescribed a four-year course leading to a certificate in English language and literature, geography, history, a foreign language, mathematics, science, drawing, manual work, physical training and, for girls, housewifery (Board of Education, 2020).

With the passage of the 1902 Act England had finally introduced a state-provided system of secondary schooling of a kind that France had created 100 years earlier. But unlike the French *lycée*, the newly created English secondary schools were divisive institutions, logically and socially distinct from elementary schools. The bulk of their pupils were the children of middle-class parents. Also, most of them were created in the image of the old public and grammar schools. Latin mottos, school uniforms, the house system, sixth forms, compulsory games and other features of the old public schools were quickly adopted, so ensuring that they would continue to be regarded as exclusively middle-class institutions reserved for the children of a privileged elite.

By the end of the 19th century, the social conditions created by the Industrial Revolution had produced a society culturally, economically and educationally divided by class. To many intellectuals and social reformers, this situation demonstrated how 18th-century classical liberalism had degenerated into an ideological device for sustaining the wealth, status and power of one social group by relegating another, much larger group to positions of social inferiority and economic poverty. They also began to raise questions about whether classical liberalism could remain viable in the kind of democratic society that was emerging at the end of the 19th century. This inevitably gave rise to the problem of reformulating classical liberalism's view of the relationship between the individual and the state in a way that would reconcile the core liberal value of individual freedom with the values and ideals of a democratic society. The response to this need was the emergence of a new conception of liberalism that was to provide the basis for most of the educational reforms that were introduced in the 20th century.

References

Bentham, J. (2009) *An Introduction to the Principles of Morals and Legislation.* Norwich: SCM Press.

Board of Education (2020) *Regulations for Secondary Schools: From 1st August 1903 to 31st July 1904 (Classic Reprint).* London: Forgotten Books.

Maclure, S. (1986) *Educational Documents: England and Wales. 1816 to the Present Day* London: Methuen.

Smith, A. (2012) *The Wealth of Nations.* Hertfordshire: Wordsworth Editions.

7 Democracy and Education

In 1295, the borough of Old Sarum was made a parliamentary constituency with the right to elect two burgesses to the English parliament. Although, by the 14th century, it had become an uninhabited hamlet, this did not prevent the landowner from nominating seven non-resident tenants to elect two members of the House of Commons. This bizarre arrangement continued for the next three centuries, making Old Sarum the most notorious of what were scornfully referred to as 'rotten boroughs'. At the 1831 general election, 152 members of the House of Commons were chosen by fewer than 100 voters, 88 by fewer than 50, and 2 – one of which was Old Sarum – by fewer than 10. At the same election, highly populated towns, such as Manchester and Birmingham, had no Member of Parliament at all.

Even though it was blatantly obvious that the electoral system was undemocratic and corrupt, demands for reform were largely ignored. But when, in the aftermath of the French Revolution, numerous public riots and demonstrations made the pressure for reform irresistible, parliament, somewhat reluctantly, passed the Representation of the People Act (1832), subsequently known as the Great Reform Act. It abolished 56 of the rotten boroughs, created 67 new constituencies and gave parliamentary representation to the new industrial cities. It also extended the vote to small landowners, tenant farmers, shopkeepers and some householders. However, these modest reforms only enfranchised one million out of seven million adults and demands for further electoral reform continued. In 1867, a second Reform Act enfranchised artisans and part of the urban male working class, immediately doubling the size of the electorate. By 1884 it had grown to around five million. In 1918, in the face of fierce opposition, the Suffragettes won the right

DOI: 10.4324/9781003625735-7

for the women's vote. Multiple voting, which gave certain groups of people two votes, was only abolished in 1948. The first election based on the democratic principle of 'one person one vote' did not happen until 1950.

The reason why democratic reforms occurred so slowly in England is bound up with its political history. The Glorious Revolution of 1688 had put an end to the absolute power of the monarchy and paved the way for the emergence of a liberal society in which individual freedom was the highest political end. Up to the 18th century, any suggestion that a liberal society could have a democratic form of government was regarded as absurd. So, when the successive parliamentary reforms of the 19th century made democratic progress inevitable, it was only to be expected that any acceptable form of democracy would have to allow an already established form of society – a liberal society – to work. In other words, for democracy to be acceptable, it first had to be liberalised.

Initially, this task was taken up by the utilitarian philosopher James Mill (1773–1836) who, in *An Essay on Government*, argued in favour of 'representative democracy': a system of government in which people elected politicians who they could remove if they enacted laws that constrained their freedom to pursue their private interests (J. Mill, 1937) But its most influential justification came from James Mill's son, John Stuart Mill (1806–1873), in his *Considerations on Representative Government* (J. S. Mill, 1951).

J. S. Mill was an Enlightenment philosopher who was sympathetic to the view that democratic participation in political decision-making would promote the Enlightenment ideals of rational autonomy, equality and self-determination. However, he was, first and foremost, a liberal, and his commitment to democracy was always tempered by the traditional liberal fear of 'the tyranny of the majority': the fear that a democratically elected government could infringe the freedom of a minority by claiming that it was enacting 'the will of the people'. His solution to this problem was to reinterpret the classical Greek concept of democracy so as to strip it of its participatory ideals. For Mill, democracy was 'government of the people, for the people' but emphatically not 'by the people'. So, while he accepted that all should have the vote, he also insisted that individual liberty could only be protected from the brute ignorance of an uneducated working-class majority if the choice of who could actually govern was limited to those he called 'the wisest few': an intellectual elite who, by virtue of their superior intelligence and better education, were the most suitably qualified to exercise political power. By redefining the classical conception of democracy so as to make it compatible with classical liberal ideology, Mill had effectively reduced it to a method for allowing 'the people' to elect their political representatives by voting in periodic elections.

Mill's suggestion that political power should be confined to the 'highly gifted and instructed few' prompted the question of how those elected to govern should be educated. The most influential answer came from the 19th-century cultural critic and poet Matthew Arnold (1822–1888), who was the eldest son of Thomas Arnold, the headmaster of Rugby School. In a series of essays published in 1869 under the title *Culture and Anarchy*, Arnold argued that the growth of democracy meant that political power would increasingly be exercised by members of the English industrial middle class whose 'philistine' attitude to culture was leading to the erosion of all civilised values (Arnold, 1932). If they were to be adequately educated to exercise political authority, the middle class had to be taught the civilising values that are cultivated through an initiation into 'high culture', which Arnold famously defined as 'the best that has been known and said' (ibid., p.vii). Needless to say, initiation into this culture required the kind of education provided by Rugby and the other public schools to the children of the aristocratic elite. For Arnold, the education of the political leaders of the democratic future should be no different from that of political leaders of the aristocratic past.

To many 19th -century social reformers, it was obvious that while Mill's version of democracy protected the freedom of a privileged few, it did little to advance the freedom of the mass of ordinary people. By the 1870s, this concern had led many liberals to believe that there was an urgent need to reformulate liberalism's core concept of freedom, a task that was initially undertaken by the Oxford philosopher, T. H. Green (1836–1882). Although Green regarded freedom as the fundamental political value, he did not think that this gave individuals the right to pursue their own private interests free from any interference by the state. Nor did he think that the classical liberal image of the private individual as someone who existed apart from society made any sense. Instead, he shared the Greek view that human beings are essentially social animals who realise their freedom by contributing with others to the common good of their society. He further argued that, by equating freedom with laissez-faire economics, classical liberalism had created levels of poverty, injustice and exploitation that denied all but a privileged few the freedom to live the kind of life that they would find satisfying and worthwhile. For Green, then, freedom is not to be defined 'negatively', as the absence of compulsion or restraint, but 'positively', as the freedom of all individuals to realise their potential and achieve self-fulfilment. But he also argued that this positive freedom was only possible in a society that accepted its obligation to introduce laws and regulations that would restrict the freedom of some individuals in order to eliminate the social disadvantages and inequalities that were preventing others from fulfilling their potential and enhancing their freedom (Green, 2006).

By the end of the 19th century, Green's political philosophy provided the rationale for a new variant of liberalism known as 'new liberalism'. Like classical liberalism, new liberalism was committed to protecting individual freedom in the face of encroachment by the state. But while classical liberalism promoted the ideas of negative freedom, limited government and laissez-faire economics, new liberalism endorsed positive freedom, the principle of social justice and state intervention to ameliorate social and economic inequalities through state-funded public welfare services.

At the beginning of the 20th century, Green's new liberalism was adopted as the official philosophy of a reconstructed Liberal Party. So, it was only to be expected that the liberal government elected in 1906 would use the power of the state to eliminate the inequalities caused by the barriers between elementary and secondary education. The first step towards achieving this aim was taken in 1907 with the introduction of a free places scheme which compelled state-funded grammar schools to offer 25% of their places free to children in elementary schools who performed well in a psychological test designed to measure their 'Intelligence Quotient', soon to be abbreviated to 'IQ'. However, since the number of working-class children passing the IQ test far outstripped the number of available places, their access to secondary education increasingly depended on competition rather than intelligence. This not only gave rise to an ever-increasing pressure for the state to provide 'secondary education for all', it also led to the suspicion that, as well as restricting the opportunity to exercise freedom, the continuing existence of a system of 'elementary' and 'secondary' education was impeding the future development of liberal democracy. One of the most influential exponents of this view was the American philosopher John Dewey (1859–1952).

Dewey took issue with two of the assumptions underpinning J. S. Mill's version of liberal democracy: the Platonic assumption that most individuals lacked the innate intelligence to make rational political judgements; and the claim that these intellectual limitations made the democratic ideal of 'rule by the people' unrealistic. In opposition to these claims, Dewey insisted that the view of intelligence as an unevenly distributed natural endowment was little more than a contrived rationalisation for the continuing existence of an aristocratic elite. He also admitted that the democratic ideal of rule by the people presupposed a level of educational attainment that did not currently exist. But, unlike Mill, he did believe that this demonstrated the impracticality of democratic ideals; it simply indicated the failure of existing liberal democracies to live up to their educational obligations. For Dewey, this failure could not be rectified by an expansion of the old 19th-century version of liberal democracy. What was needed was a new 20th-century conception of liberal democracy that retained the aspirations and ideals that gave classical Greek democracy its initial attraction and appeal. In responding to this need Dewey formulated a modernised account of Greek democracy that took account of the massive expansion of knowledge produced by modern science, particularly the theory of evolution advanced by Charles Darwin in *On the Origin of Species* (2019).

Dewey fully accepted Darwin's thesis that prehistoric humans had, like other animals, gradually developed behavioural traits that enabled them to eliminate conflicts between their survival needs and their natural environment. But he also acknowledged how this process of biological evolution had been superseded by the process of social evolution: the process that began when humans were able to communicate with each other about how to respond intelligently – rather than instinctively – to the conflicts and difficulties that arose when they started to live together in complex social communities. Like other animals, humans had previously settled their conflicts by fighting and physical force. But by developing their ability to engage in collective rational discussion – an ability Dewey called 'social intelligence' – they were now able to settle their disagreements by arriving at collectively agreed decisions about how to reconcile their differences in ways that would serve the common good.

By 'social intelligence', then, Dewey was not referring to some innate individual endowment but to a human problem-solving tool that had evolved to resolve disagreements that arose at times of social conflict and cultural change. For Dewey, it was the continuous application of social intelligence to social and cultural problems that drives the progressive development of a society in which all individuals are free to collectively contribute to the common good. For this reason, he interpreted individual freedom and social evolution as mutually dependent elements within a never-ending process of 'growth': a process through which individuals progressively develop their social intelligence by simultaneously reconstructing themselves and their society in ways that are conducive to the ever-expanding growth of their individual freedom and the pursuit of their society's common good. 'Growth' is thus a dynamic process of self-transformation and social change: an endless spiral whereby individuals, in the course of remaking their society, remake themselves. A society that seeks to expand and enlarge the growth of all its members is what Dewey understood as a democracy.

At the end of the 19th century, the political and economic conditions produced by the Industrial Revolution had made the emergence of this kind of democracy a real possibility. In *The Public and Its Problems* (1927), Dewey described how the division of labour caused by industrialisation, together with the liberal preoccupation with the right of individuals to pursue their own private interests, had led to the disintegration of traditional forms of communal life. Prior to the 19th century, people from diverse social backgrounds were able to participate in social groups – or, as he called them, 'publics' – that occupied an autonomous 'public sphere' in which communal problems could be collectively resolved on the basis of a shared commitment to the common good. But at the same time Dewey believed that industrialisation had also created more efficient modes of production that liberated people from many time-consuming tasks and so created the conditions for a vibrant public sphere to be re-established. What prevented this was another consequence of industrialisation: the emergence of a class-divided society that kept the majority of its members in a state of abject ignorance. For Dewey the only way to overcome this was to replace mass schooling with a system of 'public' education. Without radical educational reform, attempts to recreate a viable public sphere would be frustrated, and without a viable public sphere democratic progress would be impaired.

Although liberals such as J. S. Mill and Matthew Arnold accepted that 19th-century democratic reforms had made educational change unavoidable, Dewey regarded their suggestion that this simply required extending the kind of classical education previously restricted to the aristocratic elite as superficial and naïve. Indeed, the idea that a form of education that had evolved to sustain pre-democratic societies could serve the needs of a modern industrial democracy failed to recognise that without a more democratic system of education, the democratic development of society would be severely impeded. For this reason, he thought that the continuing existence of mass schooling was a serious impediment to democratic progress. Until this was abolished, schools would continue to breed democratically undesirable attitudes, such as obedience and competition, and rely on authoritarian teaching methods, such as rote learning and the inculcation of fixed beliefs. What was also frustrating democratic progress was the restriction of education to a privileged few. This elitist view had originally been legitimised by profoundly anti-democratic philosophies that remained deeply ingrained in the Western educational tradition and were still operating to hamper the practical realisation of democratic ideals. For Dewey a prerequisite to the democratic reconstruction of the Western educational tradition was the democratic reconstruction of educational philosophy, an intellectual task he brilliantly carried out in what is undoubtedly the most important and influential educational text of the 20th century: *Democracy and Education* (1916).

He began this task by assessing the strengths and weaknesses of the educational philosophies inherited from Plato and Rousseau. Although he conceded that Plato had correctly recognised the crucial role of education in creating and sustaining a certain kind of society, Dewey thought that his educational philosophy suffered from two major flaws: his portrayal of human reason as an innate endowment restricted to a fortunate few; and his failure to understand how individuals and societies simultaneously evolve and change. What Dewey most admired about Rousseau was his impassioned desire to remove the constraints on human freedom imposed by a corrupt and inequitable society. Also, while he agreed with Rousseau's emphasis on the educational significance of the child's natural needs and interests, his view of 'nature' as antithetical to 'society' created the image of a mythological 'Noble Savage' who could spontaneously flourish outside civilised society. For Dewey, Rousseau's plea to 'leave everything to nature' ignores how the child's natural capacities can only develop in a deliberately constructed educational environment in which its intelligence can be socialised by participating in shared inquiries, deliberative reasoning and collective decision-making. An educational environment that puts the power of social intelligence to full use in this way is not one that prepares individuals for future life in a democracy but one that is itself democratically organised. As Dewey famously put it, 'education is not preparation for life; education is life itself' (1897, p.78).

For Dewey, then, schools in a democracy should themselves be democratic communities, promoting the kind of social intelligence that is the prerequisite to individual freedom and growth. Since children only learn to understand themselves as democratic citizens by becoming members of a community in which the problems of communal life are resolved through collective deliberation and a shared concern for the common good, a democratic school is a common school to which children of different races, classes, genders and religions are initiated into the democratic culture embedded in the 'public sphere' characteristic of pre-industrial societies. It is only by schools' creating such a culture that children will develop the kind of social attitudes and dispositions that enable them to collectively confront their shared problems and common concerns. And it is only by enabling children to participate in such problem-solving activities that schools can promote the growth of social intelligence that the development of a more democratic society requires.

Dewey insisted that this kind of democratic school could only function if the rigid distinction between traditional and progressive approaches to teaching and learning was abolished. In *The Child and the Curriculum* (2008) he argued that the main problem with traditional teaching methods such as direct instruction and rote learning was that they taught an academic curriculum that was divorced from the interests and experiences of the child. As a result, they focused almost exclusively on children passively absorbing pre-packaged knowledge that offered little more than an endless mass of information and facts. But while traditional teaching focused too much on *what* was being taught and not enough on *who* was being taught, the problem with progressive teaching was the reverse: it was so 'child-centred' that it ignored the need for a curriculum that incorporated the established knowledge that children needed to be taught if their social intelligence was to develop and grow. As Dewey puts it, 'the belief that all genuine education comes about through experience does not mean that all experiences are genuinely or equally educative' (Dewey, 1963 p.20). What it means is that children's present experiences can only be 'educative' insofar as they can be related to a selected body of curriculum knowledge that enables them to develop those experiences in ways that will promote their future intellectual growth.

Dewey was no idealist, and he readily conceded that his theories needed to be tested in an actual school setting. To this end, he started an experimental school at the University of Chicago, where he was head of the Department of Philosophy, Psychology and Education from 1894 to 1904. He saw his school as a scientific laboratory, staffed with college-trained teachers and devoted to research, experiment and innovation. From the outset, he expected his school to perform three functions: first, to conduct experiments designed to evaluate his educational theories in actual classroom settings; second, to use the findings of these experiments to develop an established body of curriculum knowledge; and third, to develop teaching methods and curriculum content that, by relating this knowledge to children's interests and experiences, would be educative. But his long-term ambition for his laboratory school was always to provide the impetus for educational reforms that would eventually lead to a more democratic society.

Dewey's *Democracy and Education* stands alongside Plato's *Republic* and Rousseau's *Émile* as one of the canonical texts of the Western educational tradition. It has had an immense impact on modern educational thinking and inspired 20th-century educational reformers such as W. H. Kilpatrick (1871–1965), Maria Montessori (1870–1952) and Paulo Freire (1921–1997). It also influenced the English socialist historian R. H. Tawney, whose policy document 'Secondary Education for All' – written for the British Labour Party in 1922 – argued that that the continuing division between elementary and secondary schools had become democratically indefensible and should be replaced by a unified system, with primary and secondary education organised as two stages in a single continuous process (Tawney, 1922). Sixteen years later, Tawney's view was endorsed by the Spens Report on secondary education (1938), which proposed a tripartite system of secondary education consisting of 'grammar', 'technical' and 'modern' schools – a proposal that was implemented in the Education Act of 1944.

Under the terms of the 1944 Act, elementary education was finally abolished and replaced by an education system organised in three progressive stages: primary education, secondary education and further education. Secondary education was to be provided by, 'grammar', 'technical' and 'modern' schools, with selection determined by intelligence tests. However, throughout the 1950s psychologists increasingly questioned the very idea of innate intelligence and began to acknowledge that the results of IQ tests were heavily distorted by social influences and cultural bias. In 1957, the British Psychological Society published *Secondary School Selection*, which presented the results of its inquiry into the validity of the IQ tests used to legitimise secondary school selection procedures (Vernon, 2019). It concluded that the theorical rationale for IQ tests was scientifically unsound and that using them to measure children's innate intelligence was no longer credible. These psychological criticisms were reinforced by a series of sociological studies showing how the selective system systematically discriminated against children of working-class origin and that academic performance was largely determined by social and cultural factors. In short, they made it clear that, in the late 1950s, the educational opportunities for working-class children were not much different from what they had were before the tripartite system was introduced.

These psychological and sociological criticisms prepared the ground for the publication of a series of government reports that were to radically transform all aspects of the English educational system. One the first of these was the Newsom report, *Half our Future* (1963), that looked at the education of 'pupils of average or less than average ability between the ages of 13 and 16'. In a sentence that could have been written by John Dewey, it declared that 'all children should have an equal opportunity of acquiring intelligence and of developing their talents and abilities to the full' (p.iv). This reference to 'acquiring intelligence' was of immense significance. It not only acknowledged that the concept of a predetermined fixed intelligence was now officially discredited; it also reflected a growing realisation that the time had finally come to reorganise secondary education in accordance with the 'comprehensive' principle of non-selective schooling.

Following its election in 1964, the Labour government published *The Organisation of Secondary Education* (DES, 1965) announcing its intention to 'end selection and eliminate separatism in secondary education' (ibid. para.1). Over the next decade, as comprehensive reorganisation gathered pace, the division between 'modern', 'technical' and 'grammar' schools was more or less eroded. This meant that primary schools no longer had to prepare children for grammar school selection tests and were free to adopt new forms of curriculum, more progressive styles of teaching and more child-centred approaches to learning. These developments were given the official stamp of approval in the Plowden report, *Children and their Primary Schools* (CASE, 1967), which famously stated that 'one of the main educational tasks of the primary school is to build on and strengthen children's intrinsic interest in learning and lead them to learn for themselves rather than from fear of disapproval or desire for praise' (ibid. p.196).

Another Labour government commitment was to carry out a massive expansion of higher and university education. In 1963, *The Robbins Report on Higher Education* had recommended an expansion in university provision so as to give all those who are suitably qualified the opportunity for higher education. (Committee on Higher Education, 1963) It also suggested that the Teacher Training Colleges set up in the 19th century to prepare elementary school teachers should be renamed 'Colleges of Education' with sufficient independence to develop as 'educational – rather than just 'training' – institutions, preparing student-teachers to be professional educators whose work would be governed by educational values rather than non-educational pressures and political constraints. To this end, the structure and content of teacher education courses changed. Formal lectures were replaced by seminars and tutorials and courses on educational philosophy were introduced to give students an understanding of the progressive ideas of Rousseau, Froebel, Pestalozzi and Dewey. In addition, student teachers were taught the psychological principles of child development and an understanding of the sociological and historical factors affecting the ways in which present day education had developed and evolved.

By the 1970s, the old idea of the teacher as someone who imposed discipline, order and control had given way to an image of teachers as autonomous professionals, making informed judgements about what and how they should teach on educational grounds. With this enhanced level of professional independence, comprehensive schoolteachers began to replace rote learning, direct instruction and other traditional teaching methods with discovery methods, problem-solving activities and collaborative group projects. Primary schools replaced didactic teaching methods with more 'child-centred' approaches and the traditional academic curriculum was replaced by an 'integrated' curriculum in which play, spontaneity, imagination and creativity were given the central place. In the aftermath of the Robbins Report, there was a major expansion of higher education, changing it from elite system that limited access to a privileged few to a system that was accessible to all. By the beginning of the 1980s the need to educate *all* children to participate in democratic life had become a cornerstone of educational policy and the guiding principle of educational reform. To many it was seen as the dawn of a new age in which the system of mass schooling inherited from the 19th century would finally be replaced by a system of public education that would prepare all children to participate in a more open, diverse and inclusive democratic society.

It would be a mistake to think that the progressive educational reforms of the 1960s and 1970s were the result of an abrupt change to educational ideas and beliefs. Rather, they are best understood as the latest stage in the much longer and larger historical process through which the Western educational tradition developed and evolved. The first stage occurred during the 18th century when, under the influence of Enlightenment ideas, the educational beliefs, practices and institutions inherited from the past were deemed to be no longer appropriate. Stage two began when philosophical texts that had previously been deferred to without question were superseded by the philosophical works of Immanuel Kant, Jean-Jacques Rousseau and other Enlightenment philosophers. In stage three, 19th-century educational reformers such as Froebel and Pestalozzi devised and popularised a range of progressive educational teaching methods that gave practical expression to the educational philosophy articulated in Rousseau's *Émile*. The fourth stage occurred when another Enlightenment philosopher, John Dewey, subjected Plato's *Republic* and Rousseau's *Émile* to critical revision and, on this basis, constructed a modern educational philosophy appropriate to the needs and aspirations of 20th-century liberal democracies. It was only in the 1960s, when Dewey's educational philosophy began to be absorbed into the Western educational tradition, that more progressive beliefs and practices started to enter the mainstream of educational policy and practice and become formally embedded in the institutionalised framework of schools. And it is only when the Western educational tradition had reached this stage in its evolution that it became possible to appreciate the inadequacies and limitations of educational beliefs and practices inherited from the past, and so understand the history of the tradition in a different way.

It goes without saying that at every stage of this process, progressive educational change was resisted and opposed. Throughout the 19th century, it was frustrated and delayed by the introduction of a state system of mass schooling. It continued to be resisted and impeded by a privileged elite who, even in the late 20th century, clung to the 19th-century belief that there was no need to cultivate amongst the lower orders the rational intelligence that they so prized amongst themselves. This sentiment found intellectual expression in the continuing argument about whether extending education to all would vulgarise its content and lead to a lowering of academic standards. Those who engaged in this argument related to the Western educational tradition in different ways. Some, such as the essayist and literary critic T.S. Eliot (1888–1965) showed an unqualified allegiance to what, within the tradition, had hitherto been thought said and done (Eliot, 1948). Others, such as the Labour politician Anthony Crosland (1918–1977), sought to modify the tradition in order to redirect it in more progressive and democratic ways (Crosland, 2006). But although those participating in these arguments adopted fundamentally different viewpoints, their differences and disagreements were always articulated from *within* the tradition and hence were the kind of arguments that enabled it to evolve.

Prior to the 1980s, these arguments were largely conducted in a variety of institutional forums, such as assemblies, seminars, conferences and other meeting places, that allowed diverse members of the educational community to collectively discuss and rationally resolve their educational concerns. At their best, these discussions drew on a combination of rational argument, practical experience and theoretical insight in a way that allowed the conflicting views of teachers, politicians, parents, local and national government, academics and other groups with a legitimate interest in education to be acknowledged, and their differences and disagreements consensually resolved.

But over the past half-century these institutionalised settings have been systematically dismantled under the impact of an all-pervading political and economic philosophy that has systemically rejected the Western educational tradition and removed its adherents to the margins of contemporary culture. Within this contemporary culture, the rival voices of the tradition's classical and progressive protagonists have been largely expunged from official educational debate and the understanding of education embodied in the tradition has not so much been extended or refined as dismantled and disowned. As a result, schools, universities and other educational institutions are now governed by a view of education that is rarely formulated or defended, that serves no intrinsically educational purpose and is only remotely concerned with developing the human ability to reason. The result is that education is no longer what it once was, and what was once thought to be education has to some large degree disappeared. How did this come about? The answer to this question is to be found in the history of how, in the 20th century, a revised version of 19th-century classical liberalism was plucked from the shadows of relative obscurity to become the guiding doctrine of modern culture. And it only by recounting this history that it will be possible to fully appreciate the degeneration to which the Western educational tradition has proved liable.

References

Arnold, M. (1932) *Culture and Anarchy*. Cambridge: Cambridge University Press.

Board of Education. (1938) *Secondary Education.* London: HMSO.

Central Advisory Council for Education. (1967). *Children and their Primary Schools*. London: HMSO.

Committee on Higher Education. (1963) *Higher Education Report*. London: HMSO.

Crosland, A. (2006) *The Future of Socialism*. London: Little, Brown Book Group.

Darwin, C. (2019) *On the Origin of Species.* London: Natural History Museum.

Department of Education and Science. (1965) *The Organisation of Secondary Education* (Circular 10/65) London: HMSO.

Dewey, J. (1897) *My Pedagogic Creed.* School Journal, vol. 54, pp.77–80.

Dewey, J. (1916) *Democracy and Education*. New York: The Free Press.

Dewey, J. (1927) *The Public and its Problems.* New York: Henny.

Dewey, J. (1963) *Experience and Education* New York: Collier.

Dewey, J. (2008) *The Child and the Curriculum*. New York: Cosimo Classics.

Eliot, T. S. (1948) *Notes towards a Definition of Culture.* London: Faber and Faber.

Green, T. H. (2006) *Liberal Legislation and Freedom of Contract.* London: Routledge.

Mill, J. (1937) *An Essay on Government.* Cambridge: Cambridge University Press.

Mill. J. S. (1951) 'Considerations on Representative Government', in H. B. Acton (ed.) *Utilitarianism, Liberty and Representative Government.* London: Dent and Sons.

Tawney, R. H. (1922) *Secondary Education for All.* London: The Labour Party/George Allen & Unwin Ltd.

Vernon P. E. (ed.) (2019) *Secondary School Selection: A British Psychological Society Inquiry*. London: Routledge Library Editions.

8 Education Today

The Demise of the Western Educational Tradition

In 1938, 26 intellectuals attended an academic colloquium held in Paris to discuss the demise of classical liberalism and the growing popularity of T. H. Green's new liberalism. The main aim of the colloquium was to analyse the causes and consequences of classical liberalism's decline and consider how it could be modified to make it more acceptable to modern Western democracies. To this end, it produced a revised version of liberalism that combined classical liberalism's commitment to a free market economy with new liberalism's promise to remove impediments to individual freedom through state intervention. To distinguish this revised version, one of the colloquium participants – the French economist Louis Marlio – coined the term 'neoliberalism'. Nine years later, another participant, the Austrian-born economist and political philosopher Friedrich Hayek (1889–1992), invited 39 scholars, mostly economists, to the Swiss village of Mont Pèlerin to discuss how neoliberalism could be developed and strengthened in the aftermath of the Second World War. In April 1947, Hayek formally established the Mont Pèlerin Society, a community of academics who would meet on a regular basis to develop and defend neoliberal ideas (Caldwell, 2022).

As an economic theory, neoliberalism was grounded in the belief that human freedom can best be realised in a society that embraces the principles and practices of a free market. At the same time, it accepted the new liberal argument that the opportunity for all people to exercise freedom requires the state to provide education, healthcare, pensions and other welfare services. However, it strongly resisted any suggestion that these services should be owned by the state on the grounds that this would prevent them from being exposed to market

DOI: 10.4324/9781003625735-8

forces. As a political theory, neoliberalism modified the classical 19th-century view of democracy to align it with free market principles. From a neoliberal perspective, democracy's main attraction was that it offered an efficient method of allowing voters to choose between competing members of the political elite in much the same way they, as customers in a market economy, make their choices of good and services. For neoliberals, democratic citizens are to be understood as 'consumers' and democratic participation as a form of consumer choice.

Hayek set up the Mont Pèlerin Society as an independent academic community confined to developing the philosophical argument for neoliberal principles and, even today, it claims to have no official views, receive no political funding and be unaligned to any political party. However, this has not prevented its leading members from using large donations from conservative organisations, private foundations, banks, industrialists and business entrepreneurs to fund a global network of 'think tanks': non-governmental organisations undertaking research designed to promote neoliberal economic and social policies. Some of the most influential of these are the Institute of Economic Affairs, set up in 1955 to promote free-market responses to economic and social problems; the Adam Smith Institute, established in 1977 to spread the intellectual argument for the privatisation of state-owned industries; and the Centre for Policy Studies, co-founded by conservative politicians Sir Keith Joseph and Margaret Thatcher in 1974 to challenge the post-war economic consensus in Britain.

By the 1970s neoliberalism had evolved into a coherent political movement supported by an international network of alliances between think tanks, politicians, academics, journalists, businesspeople, publishers and pressure groups – all advancing the neoliberal argument for deregulating the economy and privatising state-owned public services. Initially, these arguments were confined to the fringes of mainstream political debate, but when a combination of economic stagnation, increasing unemployment, high inflation and mounting public debt began to erode confidence in orthodox economic policies, the intellectual case for a neoliberal alternative began to be embraced by conservative politicians in Britain, the United States and many other Western countries (Harvey, 2007). On 3 May 1979, Britain elected Margaret Thatcher (1925–2013) to lead a Conservative government with a mandate to curb trade union power, reduce inflation and put an end to the economic stagnation that had enveloped the country for the preceding decade. By the end of her tenure as Conservative prime minister in 1990, successive conservative governments had introduced a comprehensive range of neoliberal policies, most of which have remained unaltered to the present day.

Many of these policies were designed to apply market principles to state-provided public services. In the field of education, the government formulated an educational strategy designed to overturn the progressive educational consensus of the 1960s and 1970s and make schools more susceptible to market forces, more responsive to parental choice and more focussed on the needs of industry. Three months after being elected, the government began to implement this strategy by removing the legal obligation for local education authorities to reorganise secondary education along comprehensive lines and reinstating their right to select pupils for grammar schools on the basis of IQ tests. Further legislation was passed a year later to establish the 'Assisted Places Scheme', which allowed able pupils from state primary schools to transfer to private schools and have their fees paid by the state. The government also gave serious consideration to the Institute of Economic Affairs proposal for increasing parental choice by introducing a state-funded Voucher Scheme that would create an internal market in which parents, as consumers, used government vouchers to choose the schools that offered the 'best buy' for their children's education. Although, in principle, the government was attracted to the idea of a voucher scheme, it reluctantly concluded that, in practice, it would be too difficult to implement.

The Assisted Places Scheme was the first step towards developing forms of selection and differentiation that would provide alternatives to comprehensive education without appearing to favour a privileged elite. The next step came in 1982 with the launch of the Technical Vocational Education Initiative (TVEI), which provided government funding for schools to introduce a vocational education that would prepare non-academic students between the ages of 14 and 18 for the world of work. Technical Vocational Education Initiative courses were to constitute 30% of the students' curriculum, with the remaining 70% being the same as that being offered to non-TVEI students. Unusually, the initiative was not operated by the Ministry of Education but by the government agency responsible for workforce planning: the Department of Employment and Manpower Services. It ended in 1997 but still remains the biggest curriculum development programme ever undertaken in Britain, with a total cost in excess of £1 billion.

Another aim of the government's educational strategy was to do away with the progressive consensus that still prevailed in the various institutions and groups that made up the educational community. To achieve this aim, it set about defusing opposition from what it derisively referred to as 'the educational establishment' – the teaching profession, local and national educational inspectors and advisors, university academics and teacher educators. It therefore came as no surprise when in, 1982, the government abolished the Schools Council, an independent national forum that had been set up in 1964 to allow representatives of central government, local authorities, teachers' organisations, employers, further and higher education, parents and examining bodies to discuss the kind of curriculum content. teaching methods and assessment procedures that schools should adopt at a time of rapid social and cultural change. To fill the vacuum, the government established the School Curriculum Development Committee, whose members were appointed by, and answerable to, the Secretary of State for Education.

Another government target was the teaching profession. Throughout the 1970s, conservative politicians had argued that the progressive educational ideas embraced by the teaching profession had led to a fall in standards, politicised the curriculum, prevented the exercise of choice and created a gulf between what parents and industry wanted and what schools actually provided. They further argued that, by cultivating an image of themselves as dedicated professionals acting in the educational interests of their students, teachers had concealed the extent to which they, like all public sector professions, always exercised their professional power to protect and advance their own private interests. It was therefore only to be expected that when the government's White Paper on Teaching Quality was published in 1983, it lacked any recognition of teachers as professional educators who make the educational quality of their teaching their overriding professional concern. Instead, it simply adopted the language of the market to create an image of teachers as the 'producers' of educational goods and services with parents and students as their 'customers' (DES, 1983). In this view, education was a commodity and teaching quality was simply a measure of how effectively teachers 'delivered' it. By portraying teachers as little more than operatives in a delivery system, the White Paper on Teaching Quality reduced teaching to the means for achieving learning objectives that were themselves never examined from an educational point of view. It is therefore unsurprising that the document gave no consideration to questions about the kind of values that should determine how the quality of teaching as an *educational* process is to be understood.

As well as advancing this instrumental view of teaching, the White Paper on Teaching Quality also proposed that the organisation and content of teacher education should no longer be left to the professional discretion of universities and colleges of education but placed firmly under political control. To this end, in 1984, the government established the Council for the Accreditation of Teachers (CATE), with the power to approve, manage and accredit all aspects of teacher education courses. (MacIntyre, 1991). Over the next decade, it produced a constant stream of 'guidance' and 'directives' that would further increase government surveillance and deprive universities and colleges of any distinctively educational role. Steps were also taken to open up the teacher training 'market' to alternative providers, all offering a 'route' to Qualified Techer Status that utilised a school-based model of training and a skill-based model of assessment. An early example was the 1989 Partnership Management of Teacher Training scheme that allowed schools, as customers, to purchase a teacher training programme from a provider – usually, but not always, a university. Another was the 1993 School-Centred Initial Teacher Training (SCITT) scheme, in which the government – as customer – paid schools – as providers – to recruit trainee teachers and provide most of their training through a short period of apprenticeship to a practising 'master teacher'.

By the end of 1990s, the aspiration to provide student teachers with a professional education had been superseded by an 'apprenticeship' model of teaching training that emphasised learning practical classroom skills and techniques through 'on the job' experience. Needless to say, courses in the philosophy and history of education that had been an essential part of university and college-based courses were removed from the teacher education curriculum on the grounds that they offered little more than 'irrelevant theory' that flew in the face of ordinary common sense. Henceforth, the kind of 'theoretical' questions discussed in such courses – questions about the educational values that should inform aspiring teachers' decisions about what and how to teach – no longer needed to be discussed because they no longer needed to be asked.

The most significant legislative development of this period was undoubtedly the 1988 Education Reform Act. Part of its purpose was to introduce market competition between schools in the belief that this would increase parental choice, drive-up standards and ensure value for money. Echoing the 19th-century system of payment by results, the Act introduced 'Local Management of Schools' (LMS) that made a school's income dependent on the number of pupils it attracted, so creating an educational 'market' where schools compete with one another for students and government funding, in the same way as businesses compete with each other for customers, sales and profits. It also devolved control of school budgets to governors and head teachers, which further encouraged schools to operate as small businesses that have to be managed effectively and efficiently in order to survive. The neoliberal obsession with creating an educational market was also evident in the Act's proposals to create a quasi-independent network of state schools that would compete with ordinary comprehensive schools. This would consist of city technology colleges, grant maintained schools, faith schools and other specialist 'academies', all to be funded by the state but modelled on private fee-paying schools.

If one part of the 1988 Act was about deregulating the educational system in accordance with neoliberal principles, another part was about introducing a subject-dominated National Curriculum that that had to be followed in all state schools. This consisted of three 'core' subjects (English, mathematics and science) and seven 'foundation' subjects (technology, a modern foreign language, history, geography, art, music and physical education). The Act also introduced age-related attainment targets that were to be measured by 'Standard Attainment Tests' (SATS), taken by all children at the age of 7, 11, 14 and 16. Every school's SATS results had to be published annually in league tables so that parents could compare how effectively each school was 'delivering' the National Curriculum. The Secretary of State for Education was given unprecedented power to modify or change the programmes of study included in the curriculum as well as the statutory regulations governing all aspects of testing and assessment.

One other provision of the Act is worth noting. In a brief – and barely noticed – paragraph, the Act abolished the two Central Advisory Councils for Education (CACE) that had been set up in 1944 to advise the Minister of Education on a range of educational matters in England and Wales. Council members represented a diverse range of people from across the education community who, despite their different educational views, were able to reach a broad consensus in support of innovative educational changes that were previously considered radical by the educational establishment. Predictably, the government offered no justification for abolishing the Councils. Nor was there any proposal to replace them with another advisory body that would draw on the wide-ranging knowledge and experience offered by the educational community. Instead, in the Education (Schools) Act of 1992, it set up a new Office for Standards in Education, soon to be abbreviated to 'Ofsted', to carry out regular inspections of all state schools and to publish reports that measured their effectiveness in achieving prescribed standards of attainment by using a seven-point scale ranging from 'excellent' to 'very poor'. The similarities between Ofsted inspections and the 19th-century system of inspection introduced by the Revised Code of 1862 are not difficult to discern.

The 1988 Education Act was just one of an enormous number of educational policies introduced by successive Conservative governments that effectively put the English educational system under the control of politicians and civil servants operating through centralised bureaucracies and other unelected bodies. In line with its strategy for preventing these policies from being exposed to critical scrutiny or rational debate, the independent public and professional organisations that had acted as centres of opposition and dissent had, by the end of the century, been either emasculated or abolished. Discussion and consensus had been replaced by ideological assertion and political manipulation, and contentious educational questions about educational aims and values were largely ignored.

Since the passage of the 1988 Act, many other educational changes – ranging from those made to the organisation and funding of universities to those made to the system of post-compulsory education – could be cited. But it is hardly necessary. Nobody can doubt that the sheer volume of policies implemented during the 1980s and 1990s has left education so thoroughly infected by neoliberal ideology that it is now unremarkable for it to be characterised as a commodity 'delivered' by teachers to children and parents. Perhaps the most pernicious effect of these policies has been to make it necessary for those who still subscribe to the ideals of the Western educational tradition to conduct their discussions and debates in a culture that has excluded the questions raised in such discussions from the contemporary educational debate. But it would be a mistake to infer from this that the Western educational tradition has now totally succumbed to the prevailing neoliberal culture – for it still retains the allegiance of a variety of parents, teachers and other educational professionals, not all of whom are aware of the tradition from whence their understanding of education derives. This explains why large sections of the educational community still accept modes of educational practice that only make sense in terms of the values and beliefs embedded in the tradition. It also explains why schools, universities and other educational institutions are still only able to defend that which makes them genuinely *educational* institutions by engaging in the kind of arguments that sustain the tradition and through which it develops and evolves.

So even though it has now been marginalised and disowned, the Western educational tradition continues to exert an influence on contemporary educational practice, albeit often in a disguised or fragmented form. But because those who still retain an allegiance to the tradition are now compelled to advance its claims within an institutionalised educational framework informed by the assumptions and beliefs of neoliberalism, it is not uncommon for them to be dismissed as fanciful idealists whose educational views are outdated and irrelevant to our own modern times. Can this criticism be rejected? Is the gap between present educational realties and what would have to occur for the ideals embedded in the tradition to again become a central feature of educational debate too great to be actually bridged?

Any response to this criticism needs to be tempered by the fact that those most prone to make it are generally those who pride themselves upon their pragmatic common sense, who look to education to deliver outputs that are immediate, predictable and measurable. They are those who are so thoroughly imbued with the ethos of the age that they remain oblivious to the distinction between education and schooling and can only value education as a means to something other than education itself. It may therefore be that the gap between current educational realities and the ideals of the Western educational tradition may furnish a measure not of the unrealistic aspirations of the tradition's adherents but of the extent to which those who positively embrace contemporary neoliberal reality cannot even recognise the kind of fundamental questions to which their own impoverished understanding of education gives rise. The claim that efforts to reinstate the tradition are unrealistic and outdated may therefore be best understood as an indication of the condition of those who make it, rather than an indictment of the project against which it is directed.

If this is indeed the case, then it becomes clear that the difficult task now facing the Western educational tradition's contemporary adherents is to find ways to give dialogue and debate about the present state and future prospects of education a central place in a neoliberal culture which has replaced rational educational debate with a series of rhetorical techniques deployed by politicians to further their vested interests and disguise their ideological goals. What would this require? The first requirement is for the tradition's advocates to recreate the kind of institutional forums within which they can discuss questions about how education in the 21st century ought to be organised and conducted, where rival viewpoints are not illegitimately suppressed and where differences and disagreements are accorded full recognition. But a second requirement is that this acceptance of the legitimacy of differences, disagreements and rival viewpoints does not blind participants to the importance of their shared commitment to the core educational values and beliefs that define their allegiance to the tradition and without which they would be unable to agree about what it is they disagree about. Without this commitment, participants could not disagree in the way they do, their arguments would be rendered sterile and the Western educational tradition would disintegrate and disappear.

References

Caldwell, B. (ed.) (2022) *Mont Pèlerin 1947: Transcripts of the Founding Meeting of the Mont Pèlerin Society*. Stanford CA: Hoover Institution Press.

Department of Education and Science. (1983) *White Paper: Teaching Quality*. London: HMSO.

Harvey, D. (2007) *A Brief History of Neoliberalism*. Oxford: Oxford University Press

Macintyre, G. (1991) *Accreditation of Teacher Education; The Story of CATE 1984–1989*. London: Falmer.

9 Conclusion

Reclaiming Education for Today

This book has argued that education today can only be made intelligible by understanding the history of the tradition through which it has been conveyed to us in its present form. To substantiate this argument, it has provided a brief history of education from prehistoric times to the present day. This history began by describing how education as a self-conscious human activity first emerged towards the end of the Palaeolithic Age in an attempt to intervene in the natural processes of child-rearing and socialisation. It then explained how, in the intellectual climate pervading ancient Athens during the fifth century BC, the three leading Greek philosophers – Socrates, Plato and Aristotle – argued that the distinctive purpose of education was to cultivate the human ability to reason, and how this conception of education came to constitute the inherited pattern of thought and action we refer to as the Western educational tradition. Attention was then focused on how, in the course of its historical evolution, this tradition was Romanised, Christianised, humanised, liberalised and democratised, with particular emphasis being given to some of the influential philosophers whose ideas and arguments were to redirect the course of the tradition's development.

Consideration was also given to how, during the two centuries which separate the demise of Christian education from our own modern times, the educational ideals conveyed through the Western educational tradition were *both* championed and advanced by its Enlightenment's protagonists *and* frustrated and opposed by the introduction of state systems of compulsory schooling that use education as a strategic instrument for advancing the political goals of the nation state. The book then explained why the idea of education as

DOI: 10.4324/9781003625735-9

intrinsically concerned with the cultivation of reason is incompatible with central political and economic beliefs of our own modern neoliberal culture, especially its elevation of the values of the market to a central place. From this it concluded that education today exists, virtually unrecognised, within a system of state imposed mass schooling, a system which has abandoned the values and ideals of the Western educational tradition and is primarily concerned with serving economic and other non-educational goals.

What this history has also been at pains to show is how the educational beliefs enshrined in this tradition have continuously been corrected, modified and refined through an historically extended argument about how the particular understanding of education that provides it with its point and purpose ought to be interpreted and applied. It also identified those occasions when, as well as conducting these internal arguments, the tradition's advocates have had to engage in argument and debate with those external critics who displayed an outright hostility to the conception of education to which they subscribed. By doing so, they were not only able to expose what, in light of their own understanding of education, is mistaken in their rivals' educational beliefs. They were also able to re-examine their own educational beliefs against the strongest possible objections made to them by their opponents.

Another conclusion to which this history has led is that the tradition's adherents cannot effectively challenge the arguments of its modern detractors within the kind of educational debate now prevailing in our modern neoliberal culture: a debate where the terms of the debate already determine its outcome; and the arguments of those antagonistic to neoliberalism are bluntly rebuffed as irrelevant, misguided or confused. But if those wishing to advance the claims of the Western educational tradition have to do so within the confines of a debate that prevents them from exposing neoliberal educational policies and practices to rational argument, what is to be their response? Should they reluctantly admit that the Western educational tradition has now become a thing of the past? Or should they try to find ways to subvert the hegemonic dominance of neoliberal modes of educational discourse and debate sufficiently to enable them *both* to effectively challenge neoliberal educational policies *and* to conduct their own internal dialogue about how the tradition can be made appropriate to the 21st century?

What needs to be done for such subversion to be achieved? The answer to this question suggested in this book is that it would require the tradition's contemporary adherents to undertake two distinct but related tasks. On the one hand, they would have to rebuild an autonomous public sphere that was free from state interference and within which the diverse range of people who constitute the educational community could articulate their differences and form a collective consensus about how, in the 21st century, education ought to be conducted and understood. However, in pursuing this task, it would have to be recognised that a vibrant public sphere can only survive for any length of time if it sustained through institutional forums – non-aligned societies, independent organisations, professional associations and the like – that are conducive to free and open discussion and in which all can contribute on equal terms. So, the second task is to establish and preserve enduring institutional means for a debate about education today in which there are no barriers to free and open communication and where it was recognised that rationality, far from being the preserve of a political or bureaucratic elite, was no one's property.

Much more needs to be said, of course, about what more would be required for the Western educational tradition to be restored in a 21st century form. But does the all-pervading market mentality that is now so firmly entrenched in our modern neoliberal culture make it all but impossible for the kind of reclamation being envisaged to actually occur? Fortunately, the history of this tradition provides an answer to this question. For what this makes clear is that what is being envisaged is something like a 21st century re-enactment of what happened following the Roman Empire's decline into the Dark Ages when, after facing something approaching virtual extinction, the Western educational tradition was gradually revived and restored.

One of the key historical events contributing to this revival was the emergence of *disputatio*, the formal procedure for rationally resolving disagreements that formed the basis of the scholastic system of education that dominated medieval universities from the 13th to the 16th century. What has to be remembered is that *disputationes* could only be conducted if universities provided an institutional arena in which the academic community could 'dispute' each other's arguments, ask and answer fundamental questions and test their conflicting viewpoints through rational discussion and debate. And it was in response to this need that the medieval university formally established the *seminarium*, or seminar, an academic genre that created the kind of 'public sphere' within which scholars could freely express their differences and collectively resolve their disagreements through rational dialogue and deliberation.

But what this history has also made abundantly clear is that the medieval university was very different from its contemporary counterpart. It was largely an independent, self-governing institution whose statutes and regulations protected its academic integrity from external interventions by either church or state. In contrast, modern neoliberal universities are funded and assessed on the basis of state-imposed 'performance indicators' designed to ensure that they serve the economic needs of the market. The academic curriculum of the medieval university gave pride of place to the *artes liberales*, the seven liberal arts that provided the knowledge, skills and intellectual dispositions required to participate in unconstrained argument and rational debate. The modern university, on the other hand, gives pride of place to those subjects – science, engineering, information technology and the like – that teach the kind of technical knowledge and skills that will equip students for professional and specialist occupational roles. It is therefore unsurprising that subjects such as philosophy and history – where technical knowledge and skill have no obvious application – have declined in importance and are now in the ludicrous position of having to justify their place in the academic curriculum by resorting to contrived arguments about how they make an important contribution to the professional preparation of lawyers, accountants, corporative executives and the like.

It thus turns out that the ability of contemporary universities to critically subvert neoliberal ideology has itself been subverted by their employment of the kind of ideologically infected discourse that it has been their historical purpose to rationally question and critically assess. As a result, the important questions that medieval scholars could formally and rigorously debate through the process of *disputatio* are no longer regarded as being important and have been relegated to the margins of contemporary academic debate. One particular measure of the degree to which contemporary academic discourse has uncritically absorbed neoliberal assumptions is the extent to which what can be said and done in university departments of education is now constrained by a politically imposed and state-controlled teacher training curriculum that concentrates on the acquisition of teaching competences and managerial techniques and in which the history and philosophy courses that were once an essential part of teacher education are now discouraged or proscribed. This has ensured that student teachers are deprived of the intellectual resources that previously allowed them to confront fundamental questions about the educational values that inform their decisions about what and how to teach. And by doing this, teachers' professional autonomy has been restricted to a limited technical discretion within a restrictive framework of bureaucratic inspection and political control.

But the failure of the contemporary university to emulate its medieval predecessor does not mean that those fundamentally opposed to neoliberal educational policies are now deprived of *any* independent forum within which they can engage in the kind of antagonistic dialogue that the academic status quo no longer encourages or promotes. One of the unintended by-products of the widespread opposition to neoliberal educational reforms has been the recasting of existing non-academic organisations, and the creation of digital platforms and other non-academic arenas, within which members of the educational community can come together to wage a kind of intellectual warfare against an educational system that now compels them to accept a conception of education which they cannot endorse or accept. These include teachers' professional organisations, teacher education societies, research networks, curriculum development associations, school councils, academic conferences and social media like Facebook and Bluesky. Each has its own distinctive membership and mode of participation, and each operates in accordance with their own distinctive procedures and aims. But together, they offer a set of institutionalised forums in which neoliberal assumptions and beliefs are no longer protected from systematic challenge and where attempts to revive and restore a form of education that promotes the cultivation of reason are given due recognition. What those participating in these forums are – however unwittingly or unconsciously – trying to achieve is the construction of new forms of dialogical community within which the educational ideals conveyed through the Western educational tradition can be kept alive in a society which denigrates and denies everything that the tradition proclaims and affirms.

Index

Aberlard, P. 36–7
Academy 24, 26
Adam Smith Institute 76
Agricultural Revolution 13
agoge 19
Aquinas, T. 37
arête 20, 24, 30, 38
aristoi 20–1, 24
aristokratia 20–1
Aristotle 26–9, 31
artesliberales 87
Arnold, M. 63, 66
Assisted Places Scheme (1979) 77
Augustine of Hippo 33

Bacon, F. 45
Bell, A. 55
Bentham, J. 54
Bryce Commission (1894) 58–9

cathedral schools 35–6
Christiana 41
Christian humanism 39–41
Cicero, M. T. 30, 39–40
civitas 30, 33
classical antiquity 17, 34, 38, 42
Cognitive Revolution 9, 11
Copernicus, N. 44–5
Council for the Accreditation of Teachers (1984) 79
Crossland, A. 73
cuneiform 15–16

Dark Ages 42, 86
Darwin, C. 65
democracy: ancient Greek 21–4; liberal 62–6
Democracy and Education 67–9
demokratia 21
Descartes, R. 45–6
Dewey, J. 64–72
dialectic 22, 26, 35, 37
disputatio 36–7, 42, 45, 86–7

education: emergence of 11; purpose of 2–3
Education Act (1902) 59
Education Act (1944) 69
Education Act (1988) 81
Education (Schools) Act (1992) 81
educational: community 73, 78, 81–2, 86, 88; debate 73, 81–3, 85; philosophy 4, 6
elementary education 55–8, 69
Elementary Education Act (1870) 57
Eliot, T. S. 73
Émile 48–50, 69, 72
Enlightenment 42, 46–7, 49, 51
Erasmus, D. 40
eudaimonia 26–8

French revolution 53, 54, 61
Froebel, F. 50–1

Galileo, G. 44–5
grammar schools 58–9, 64, 70, 77
grammaticus 30
Green, T. H. 63–4

habitiuation 17
Harari,Y. N. 9
Hayek, F. A.75–6
Hegel, G. W. F. 5
Homer 17–18
Homo sapiens 8–13, 47
Horkheimer, M. 5
humanism 38–9

Ignatius of Loyola 40
Iliad 18, 20
Industrial Revolution 54, 59, 66
Institute of Economic Affairs 76
intelligence: innate 65, 67; quotient 64; social 65–6, 68; tests 69
intergenerational learning 10
Ionian school 19

Jesuit schools 41

Kant, I. 46–7, 72
Kindergarten 50

laissez-faire 54, 63, 64
Lancaster, J. 55
Latin schools 39
lectio 36
Leonardo da Vinci. 38
Les Philosophes 46
liberalism: classical 54, 59, 62–4, 74–5; new 64, 75
licencia docendi 36
local management of schools 80
ludus litterarus 30

MacIntyre, A. C. 6
Marx, K. 15
Mesopotamian: cities 14–15; civilisation 14, 17, 29; gods 15; schools 16; theocracy 19
Mill, J. 62
Mill, J. S. 62–3, 65–6
monitorial system 55–6
Mont Pèlerin Society 75–76

nation states 53–4, 84
National Curriculum 80
neoliberalism 75–6, 82, 85
Newsom Report (1963) 70
Newton, I. 45
noviate 35
novicii 34–5

Odyssey 18, 20
Ofsted 81

paideia 20–1, 27, 30, 35, 38
payment by results 57, 80
Peddiwell, J. Abner 12
Pestalozzi, J. H. 50–1, 71–2
philosophia 19
phronesis 27–8
pictography 15
pietas 30, 41
Plato 24–9, 33, 51, 67, 72, 84
Plowden Report (1967) 71
polis 19–21, 24–5, 33
pubic: schools 39, 58–9; sphere 66, 68, 86
Pythagoras of Samos 19

Quintilianus, M. F. 30, 40

Ratio Studiorum 41
reason 2–3; eclipse of 5
Reform Act (1832) 61
Renaissance 38, 42, 58
The Republic 24–6
Revised Code 57, 81
Robbins Report (1963) 71
Roman education . 30, 32, 34
Rousseau, J. -J. 47–51, 67, 71–2

The Saber-Tooth Curriculum 12–13
scholasticism 37–8, 40–1
schools: democratic 68; monastic 35–6, 42; monitorial 56; public 38, 58–9
Schools Council 78

Scientific Revolution 44–6
seminarium 86
Society of Jesus 40–1
Socrates 22–6, 28–9, 31, 37
Socratic method 22–3, 26, 37
Sophists 21–2, 24
Spartan education 19–20
Spens Report (1938) 69
Studia Humanitatis 39, 41–2

Taunton Commission (1868) 58
teacher education 71, 79
Technical and Vocational Educational Initiative (1982) 77
Thales of Miletus 18
Thatcher, M. 76
trivium and *quadrivium* 35–6, 42
Twain, M. 3

university: contemporary 87–8; medieval 36–7, 39, 86–7
Uoma Universale 38–9

Western education 2, 6, 17, 24, 54
Western educational tradition 28–9, 31, 42, 51, 61, 72–4, 81–3
Whitehead, A. N. 29
White Paper: Teaching Quality (1983) 78–9
writing: invention of 15

For Product Safety Concerns and Information please contact our EU representative GPSR@taylorandfrancis.com Taylor & Francis Verlag GmbH, Kaufingerstraße 24, 80331 München, Germany

Batch number: 10398441

Printed by Printforce, the Netherlands